GW00838623

HEINEMANN HISTORY

BRITAIN
1750 to 1900

STUDY UNITS

Heinemann

John Child

Heinemann Library,
a division of Heinemann Publishing (Oxford) Ltd,
Halley Court, Jordan Hill, Oxford OX2 8EJ

OXFORD LONDON EDINBURGH MADRID
ATHENS BOLOGNA PARIS MELBOURNE
SYDNEY AUCKLAND SINGAPORE TOKYO
IBADAN NAIROBI HARARE GABORONE
PORTSMOUTH NH (USA)

First published 1992

This edition published 1995

95 96 97 98 1 2 3 4 5 6 7 8 9 10

**British Library Cataloguing in Publication Data is available
from the British Library on request.**

ISBN 0–431–07364–3

Designed by Ron Kamen, Green Door Design Ltd, Basingstoke

Illustrated by Douglas Hall and Jeff Edwards

Printed in Hong Kong

Acknowledgements

The author and publisher would like to thank the following for
permission to reproduce photographs:

The front cover shows people waiting for help in the workhouse
in a painting by Sir Luke Fildes (1874)

Agricultural Economics Unit, Oxford: 2.2D
Avon Reference Library / Rob Cousins: 2.14C
Bodleian Library: 1.1D, 4.3C
Bridgeman Art Library: 1.1H, 2.6A, 2.9B, 2.11B, 2.13B, 3.4C,
4.5A, 4.6C, 5.1A
Bridgeman Art Library / British Library: 3.6J
Bridgeman Art Library / Fitzwilliam Museum, University of
Cambridge: 1.1E
Bridgeman Art Library / Gavin Graham Gallery, London: 2.16Z
Bridgeman Art Library / House of Commons: 1.1C
Bridgeman Art Library / Royal Holloway and Bedford New
College: Cover, 2.12C, 2.16T
Bristol Museum and Art Gallery: 3.1A
British Library: 1.1F, 3.5D
British Museum: 4.1B, 4.2B
Celtic Picture Library: 2.4C
Communist Party Picture Library: 4.8J, 4.8P
Corcoran Gallery of Art, Washington DC: 3.3A
Edifice / Adrienne Hart-Davies: 5.2
Edifice / Lewis: 5.2
E.T. Archive: 4.2C
Mary Evans Picture Library: 2.1E, 2.12B, 2.13D, 2.14A, 3.2E,
3.6H, 4.7D, 4.8B, 4.8C, 4.8I
Giraudon / Bridgeman Art Library: 4.1C
Guildhall Library / Bridgeman Art Library: 1.1B, 2.9C, 2.12A,
2.14B
Michael Holford: 2.8A
Michael Holford / Science Museum, London: 2.14D
Holt Studios International: 5.2
Hulton Deutsch Collection: 2.16Q, 3.6R
Illustrated London News Picture Library: 3.4B
Institute of Agricultural History and Museum of English Rural
Life: 2.2H, 2.3C
Leeds City Council, Department of Leisure Libraries: 2.16B,
2.16E

London Transport Museum: 5.1B
Mansell Collection: 1.1G, 2.5A, 2.5C, 2.5D, 2.7C, 2.10C,
2.16L, 2.16Z, 4.2D, 4.4E, 4.8G
Merthyr Tydfil Library Service: 2.16J
Metropolitan Museum of Art, New York: 2.6D
Museum of London: 2.10B, 4.3B
National Maritime Museum, London: 3.6D
National Maritime Museum, San Francisco: 2.13A
National Monuments Record: 2.16K
National Museums and Galleries on Merseyside: 2.2G, 2.7A
National Museum of Wales: 2.4A
National Portrait Gallery: 1.1A
Natural History Museum, London: 4.6F
Peter Newark's American Pictures: 3.2B
Out of the West Publishing / Linda Mackie Collection: 2.3B
Picturepoint: 3.2D
Punch Library: 4.5B, 4.7F, 4.8O
Quadrant Picture Library: 2.13E, 5.2
Science Museum, London: 2.4D
Science and Society Picture Library: 2.16F
Skyscan: 5.2
Tate Gallery, London: 4.6G
Trustees of the Wedgwood Museum, Barlaston, Staffordshire:
2.8B, 3.6P
Trade Union Congress: 4.4C
Victoria and Albert Museum, London: 3.2C
Weidenfeld and Nicolson Ltd: 4.7E, 4.8L

Every effort has been made to contact copyright holders of
material published in this book. Any omissions will be
rectified in subsequent printings if notice is given to the
publisher.

We would also like to thank HarperCollins Ltd for permission
to use Source A on page 10, which was taken from *Agriculture
1730-1872* by J. R. S. Whiting, originally published by Evans
Brothers, 1971.

*1995 marks my tenth anniversary of working on history text books.
I would like to thank all of the staff at Heinemann who have helped
me, but, in particular, Paul Shuter and Kath Donovan, who have
made a difficult challenge, not only possible, but enjoyable.*

Details of written sources
In some sources the wording or sentence structure has been
simplified to ensure that the source is accessible.

R. J. Cootes, *Britain Since 1700*, Longman, 1968: 4.3D
C. P. Hill, *A Survey of British History*, Arnold, 1968: 4.3E
Simon Mason, *Transport and Communication 1750–1980*,
Blackwell, 1985: 2.13C
Peter Mathias, *The First Industrial Revolution*, Methuen, 1969:
2.1C
Trevor May, *An Economic and Social History of Great Britain
1760–1970*, Longman, 1987: 2.13F
Charlotte and Denis Plimmer, 'Black Ivory', an article in *The
British Empire*, (Volume 4), BBC / Time Life Books, 1971:
3.6B, 3.6C, 3.6G
Bob Rees and Marika Sherwood, *Black Peoples of the Americas*,
Heinemann, 1992: 3.6I
D. Richards and J. W. Hunt, *Modern Britain 1783–1964*,
Longman, 1965: 3.2A
Dorothy Thompson, *The Chartists*, Wildwood House, 1986.
4.8F
Cecil Woodham-Smith, *The Reason Why*, Heinemann, 1971:
3.4A

CONTENTS

1.1 Britain in 1750

Two monarchs dominated the period from 1750 to 1900. **George III** reigned from 1760 to 1820; **Queen Victoria** followed from 1837 to 1901. George III shared power with Parliament. This sharing of power had been decided by the English Civil War in the 1640s and the Revolution Settlement of 1688–9. However, we shall see that, by 1900, Parliament had become much more powerful than the monarch.

Parliament also changed between 1750 and 1900. In 1750, all MPs were landowners. In some places ordinary people could vote for MPs at elections. But there was no secret vote and people usually voted the way their landlord told them. After 1750 there was a feeling that power should be shared by everyone. The vote was gradually extended to more people by acts of parliament in 1832, 1867 and 1884. Voting by secret ballot started in 1872. By 1900 most voters were working people. The first working-class MP, Keir Hardie, was elected in 1892.

A SOURCE

George III, aged 22, in his coronation robes. He was king for 60 years. He was therefore a major figure in the events covered by the first half of this book.

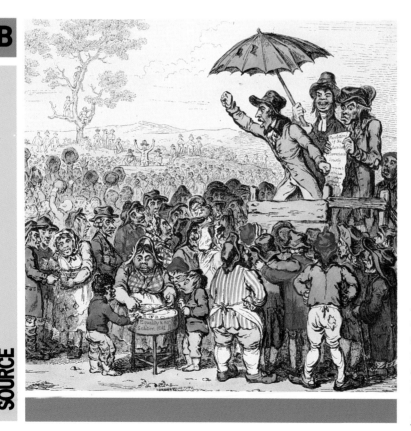

B SOURCE

A cartoon by Gillray showing an election speech. Do you think the cartoonist is trying to show an impressive picture? Some of the crowd are very excited and are waving their hats. The lady on the left is probably the reason; she is handing out free gin, paid for by one of the candidates.

Britain became bigger and more powerful between 1750 and 1900. In 1066 William the Conqueror had become King of England; after the conquest of north Wales, in 1283, Edward I had become King of England and Wales; from 1707, Scotland, England and Wales were joined as Great Britain. Then, George III saw Ireland added to his kingdom in 1801 when the **United Kingdom** was formed. The **British Empire** grew after 1750. British merchants began trading further afield. This caused competition with other European powers. Britain fought major European wars from 1756–63 and 1793–1815. British traders and British armies took possession of foreign land. Gradually a huge British Empire was formed, including land in Canada from 1763, in India from 1757 and in Australia from 1770.

The **lives of people** changed too. In 1750, people mainly lived in the **countryside**. Most land was owned by the Church or the aristocracy, like the Dukes of Norfolk or Marlborough. Only slightly less wealthy were the gentry. These were squires who owned large estates, but usually all in one county. They farmed some of their land and rented out the rest to tenant farmers. Farmers employed labourers to help them on the land. Most people in the countryside worked in farming or jobs linked to farming like blacksmiths.

A painting of Charles James Fox, MP, addressing the House of Commons in 1793. Fox was well-known as an excellent debater.

Labourers in the countryside. The smocks they are wearing were typical all over the country.

Most **towns** in 1750 were small market towns or ports. Craftspeople making and selling goods such as shoes, hats and clothes had workshops in the towns. London was by far the biggest town, with a population of about half a million. Bristol, Liverpool and Hull were important ports. Leeds, Norwich and Bath were also large towns. The wealthy enjoyed town life. There were assembly rooms for dancing and people also strolled in the pleasure gardens such as Vauxhall and Ranelagh in London. There were coffee shops and bath-houses. But some parts of the towns were very squalid. Dram houses sold cheap gin; drunkenness was common. Medical science was simple, so illness was common and treatment often painful.

Much of this also changed after 1750. **Agriculture** remained important, but farming methods changed. Some **industries**, like making cloth, saw dramatic changes with large factories springing up. More food and more jobs in factories caused large towns to grow. These towns became crowded and unhealthy. Life remained hard for the poor. Coping with their problems became a major task for the government.

This book is the story of all of these changes.

E

The Braddyll family, painted by Sir Joshua Reynolds, in 1789. The Braddylls were wealthy landowners and lived at Conishead Priory in Lancashire.

F

A tinted engraving by Rowlandson, showing a dram shop. In 1751, an Act was passed to tax spirits and drunkenness declined.

The Ranelagh pleasure gardens in London. Many of the guests are in fancy dress; some are dancing round a maypole. The house on the left is in the Queen Anne style which was very popular at the time; the other buildings show how classical arches and pillars influenced architecture at the time.

George III

George III (1738–1820) became king in 1760, at 22 years of age, when George II died of a heart attack while sitting on the lavatory. George III was not clever, but he was hard working, religious and dignified. He was a powerful political figure; no minister could survive without his support. In 1788, George III became ill. He probably had **porphyria**, a blood disease which poisons the brain. It had symptoms similar to madness. George III recovered in 1789, but the illness kept recurring. He drifted out of political life and died, grey haired and insane, when he was 81 years old.

A watercolour by Rowlandson, dated 1787. Poor diet and dental care left many people without teeth. Transplanting artificial or human teeth was one remedy. Hospitals and battlefields were the main source of supply for human teeth.

2.1 Population

In 1750 the population of Britain was about 7 million and rising slowly. The first national census, in 1801, showed that the population had reached 10.5 million. By 1851, the figure was 21 million; by 1901, 37 million. The rise was greatest in industrial towns like Birmingham, Manchester and Glasgow, but even rural counties grew. The rise was most obvious in the Midlands and North of England, South Wales and the lowlands of Scotland. Historians have argued about whether more **births** or fewer **deaths** caused the rise. Births and deaths were not recorded until 1836. Before that, the only records were baptism and burial registers kept by the Church.

A **SOURCE**

Church records show that the increase was due to a slightly rising birth rate and a much reduced death rate. People lived longer because there were better living conditions and more food; cheap gin was put out of reach by taxes. But the most important cause was babies surviving infancy, mothers surviving childbirth and people recovering from illness because of better medical care.

From 'Freedom and Revolution' by R. J. Unstead, 1972.

C **SOURCE**

The parish registers became very inaccurate after 1780. The records of burials underestimate deaths by as much as 25%. There were more births than the records of baptisms show. Historians have shown that medical changes could not have improved death rates much. Advances were patchy and costly. Living conditions in the towns got worse, not better, until about 1840. More births, caused by earlier marriage and better job prospects caused the rise.

From 'The First Industrial Nation' by Peter Mathias, 1969.

B **SOURCE**

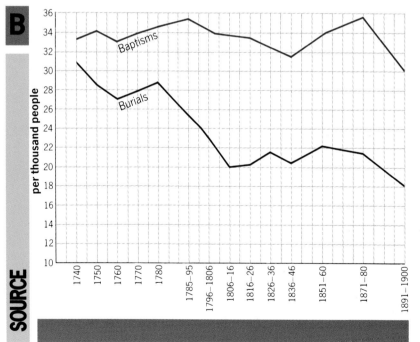

A graph showing the number of baptisms and burials from 1740–1900. These figures are taken from parish registers, records kept by busy clergymen, at a time when fewer people were going to church. Some historians don't trust these figures.

D **SOURCE**

Why has the population of Birmingham increased from 23,000 in 1750 to 30,000 in 1770? It must be because of an increase in employment. People are getting married earlier (and having more children) because the children they have do not cause them great expense. Any child, as soon as it can use its hands, can provide the family with money.

From 'Political Arithmetic' by Arthur Young, 1774.

SOURCE

The Cow Pock 1802. A cartoon by Gillray. In 1796, Edward Jenner showed that patients vaccinated with the harmless disease of cattle called 'cowpox' became immune to the deadly smallpox. Many people were very suspicious of the idea, as this cartoon shows.

The population rose rapidly until about 1880. Large families were common. After that the death rate began to fall because of better living conditions and medical care. But the birth rate fell even faster. Parents had fewer children. The size of families began to fall to the size we are used to today. The population increase slowed down.

The rise in population changed Britain. It led to overcrowding and poor **living conditions** in most cities. These cities grew rapidly; by 1900 most British people lived in **cities**. The increased population also caused changes in the British economy. More people meant more **demand** for food and other goods. Farmers and manufacturers made big **profits**. More people also meant more **workers**, so farmers and manufacturers could find plenty of labour without having to pay high **wages**. The following units describe these changes in the economy.

Malthus

The Reverend Thomas Malthus (1766–1834) was an influential writer. In 1798 he wrote *An Essay on Population*, in which he claimed the population of Britain was rising dangerously fast. The census result of 1801 seemed to prove him right.

Malthus said that food supplies would fall behind the growing population, there would not be enough jobs; poverty and starvation would follow. This was already happening in Ireland. Malthus's book caused concern and influenced political ideas. Many politicians said that it was wrong for the government to help the poor and hungry. This would allow them to have more children, making the problem worse. But Malthus was wrong. New methods of farming produced much more food; factories produced more jobs. The Industrial Revolution saved Britain from mass starvation.

2.2 The Agricultural Revolution

The traditional method of farming was called the **open field system**. It was very wasteful. The cultivated land around a village was normally divided into three great fields. Every farmer had small **strips** of land in each of the fields. Every year, all the farmers had to grow the same crops; **wheat** (for bread) in one field and **barley** (for ale) in another. Each farmer's strips were widely scattered, so it was difficult to move equipment between strips. Weeds spread from strip to strip easily, despite the **baulks** or unused pathways between them. The third field was left **fallow** (nothing grown) so that the soil could recover. Another underused area was the **common land**. This was left as a place for the villagers to gather free firewood, fruit and berries and graze their animals. This was cheap, but it made it impossible to control the breeding of the animals.

Once the **population** began to rise, there were more and more people needing food. Farmers could charge **higher prices**, make **bigger profits** and still sell all their produce. This made them keen to produce as much food as possible. To increase their produce, they changed their **methods of farming**. Landowners needed more control over their own land before they could introduce more efficient methods of farming. They started to swap strips to consolidate their land into larger units. Sometimes landowners would meet up and agree to divide the land into separate farms. This was called **enclosure**. If they could not all agree, the larger landowners could get Parliament to pass an **Enclosure Act** to force the redistribution of the land. Soon these Acts began to include the enclosure of the common land. Between 1750 and 1810, there were over 4,000 Enclosure Acts.

Once the land was enclosed, farmers could introduce new methods. Some farmers, like **Viscount Townshend**, adopted the Norfolk four course **rotation of crops**. This involved using one field for wheat, one for clover, one for barley or oats and one for turnips or swedes. These crops were swapped around the fields every year. No fields had to be kept fallow because the clover and the swedes naturally replaced the nutrients which the

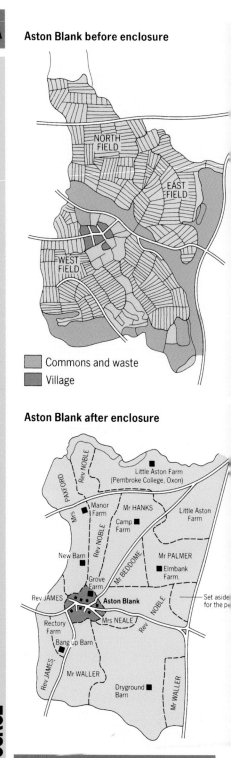

A Aston Blank before enclosure

NORTH FIELD

EAST FIELD

WEST FIELD

☐ Commons and waste
☐ Village

Aston Blank after enclosure

Rev NOBLE
Mrs PAXFORD
Little Aston Farm (Pembroke College, Oxon)
Mrs Manor Farm
Mr HANKS
Little Aston Farm
Camp Farm
Rev NOBLE
Mr BEDDOME
Mr PALMER
New Barn
Elmbank Farm.
Grove Farm
Set aside for the pe
Rev JAMES
Aston Blank
Rev NOBLE
Rectory Farm
Mrs NEALE
Bang up Barn
Rev JAMES
Mr WALLER
Dryground Barn
Mr WALLER

SOURCE

The enclosure of fields at Aston Blank, Gloucestershire, in 1752.

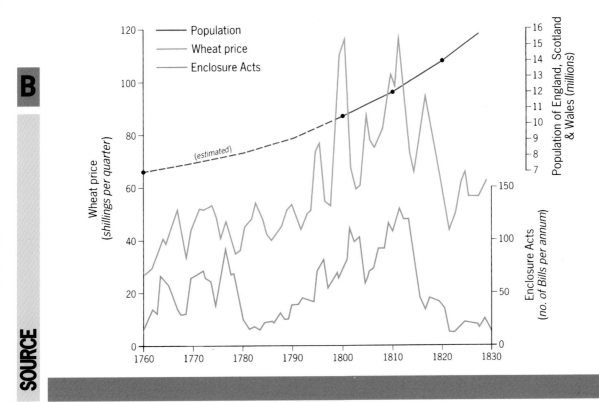

This graph shows the link between growing population, rising prices and enclosures.

wheat and barley or oats used up. The fields of clover and swedes could be used to graze animals, whose manure enriched the soil as they fattened on the crops. This produced higher yields of grain and meat.

Other farmers experimented with new machinery. **Jethro Tull** invented a **seed drill** which could be pulled along behind a horse. The drill spread the seeds evenly, in rows and then covered them up as protection against the birds. Tull later invented a **horse-drawn hoe** which could be dragged through the fields weeding between the lines of crops.

Some farmers used **selective breeding**. This involved using selected animals to develop new breeds: cattle which produced more milk and meat, sheep which gave more meat and wool. **Robert Bakewell** developed the New Leicester sheep. The **Colling brothers** bred the Durham shorthorn cattle. These animals could then be sold to farmers to breed with their own livestock, to produce improved animals.

These changes in farming had far reaching effects. The **quantity of food** produced increased. The **quality of food** also improved. This helped the population grow. But farms couldn't employ all of the extra people in the countryside; many had to move to the **towns** to find work. This was good for industry. It gave employers plenty of cheap **labour**.

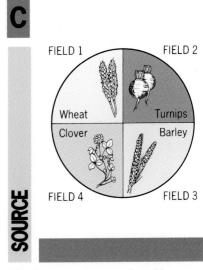

This diagram represents the fields on a farm using the four course rotation. Can you draw a diagram to show what would happen in the following year?

Not everyone benefited from the enclosures, though. Many **yeomen farmers**, who owned their own small farms, could not afford the cost. Some had to sell up and become labourers. Villagers suffered from the loss of the **common land**: the ground they sometimes got in exchange was no real compensation.

This first phase of the **agricultural revolution** came to a peak in the years between 1790 and 1810. For most of this time Britain was at war with France. Imports of cheap food from the continent were cut off. This made prices rise even faster and farmers made record profits from enclosures and new farming methods. When the war ended in 1815, cheap imports returned. For a while there was more food in Britain than its 10 million people could buy and prices fell. Farmers' profits fell and there was a period of depression in agriculture. This lasted until about 1840. By then, the population had risen to about 18 million. Prices rose again and farmers began to look for even more efficient methods to make the most of the possible profits. They started a second phase of the agricultural revolution called **high farming**.

High farming was the application of science and technology to agriculture. Many farmers began to use new machinery, new fertilizers and better drainage methods.

Machinery was introduced to save labour. For example, seed drills and threshers were used widely for the first time. From about 1850, steam power began to be used to drive farm machinery. Steam-powered reapers and threshers could do the work of many men.

 E **Wheat output in England and Wales**

1750	15m quarters
1790	19m quarters
1820	25m quarters

Notice that the biggest increase came after 1790. A quarter was one-fourth of a hundredweight of wheat (about 12.5 kilograms).

 F In 1710, the cattle and sheep sold at Smithfield Market weighed on average as follows:
cattle   370lb
sheep   28lb

Now they weigh:
cattle   800lb
sheep   80lb

Sir John Sinclair, President of the Board of Agriculture, 1795.

 D

Cotswold sheep (1866), exaggerated in size by the artist.

 G

A Lincolnshire bull painted by George Stubbs in 1790.

An 8 horse-power steam threshing machine in 1860. The machine was used to separate the seed-corn from the straw.

Better **drainage** methods stopped seed and crops rotting in the ground and so increased yields. Steam engines could pump excess water from the black silts of the fens for just 2s 6d (12p) per year. Factories could produce clay pipes for drainage trenches at a cost of less than £1 per thousand and Fowler's mole plough could lay them for less than £5 per acre.

Fertilizers were also used to increase yields. Guano (bird droppings rich in phosphates) was imported at a rate of over 100,000 tons a year from Peru in the 1850s; other natural fertilizers included crushed bones and soot. Superphosphates, nitrates and other artificial fertilizers were imported from Germany or bought from factories at home. In 1842 Sir John Lawes opened a chemical fertilizer factory in London.

As a result of these developments, farm production rose by 70% between 1840 and 1870, although the amount of farmland stayed the same. The number of farmworkers dropped by 300,000. This second phase of the agricultural revolution, from 1840 to 1870, was the **golden age** of farming. Unfortunately it didn't last long.

Townshend

Viscount Townshend (1674–1738) was a British diplomat to Europe. While in Europe, he learned about the use of clover and turnips as part of **crop rotations**. In 1730, he argued with the prime minister, Sir Robert Walpole, and retired from politics. He returned to his estates in Norfolk determined to make his farms more efficient. He made the farmers who rented his land use crop rotations which gave plenty of turnips and other winter fodder He was nicknamed 'Turnip' Townshend as a joke, but, in fact, his well publicized success made his methods popular with rich landowners.

2.3 Agricultural Depression

The 1870s was a decade of **bad weather** in Britain. Crops went mouldy in the ground; machinery was bogged down in the muddy fields. Three million sheep died of foot rot in 1879 alone.

Normally, poor output would have sent prices up and this would have cushioned the blow for farmers. But by the 1870s they had a second problem – **foreign competition**. **Steam ships** on the oceans and **railways** in foreign continents had opened up vast new areas of food production. Huge quantities of cheap grain came flooding in from the prairies of North America. Cheap wool was shipped in from Australia and New Zealand. These imports kept prices low and British farmers' profits fell badly. Hundreds of British grain and sheep farmers went bankrupt. **Refrigeration** was invented at this time, too. This enabled shiploads of frozen beef and other goods to come from New Zealand, Australia and Argentina.

A **SOURCE**

August was very unfavourable. Pastures on clay land were as wet as in the middle of winter. Grass was all trodden away and cattle sank in to their knees. The quality of both wheat and barley was wretched. No corn to sell and nobody cared to buy British produce. Vast quantities of grain pouring in from the USA. In this year, the first shipment of refrigerated beef arrived in Britain.

From the official Agricultural Records for 1879.

B **SOURCE**

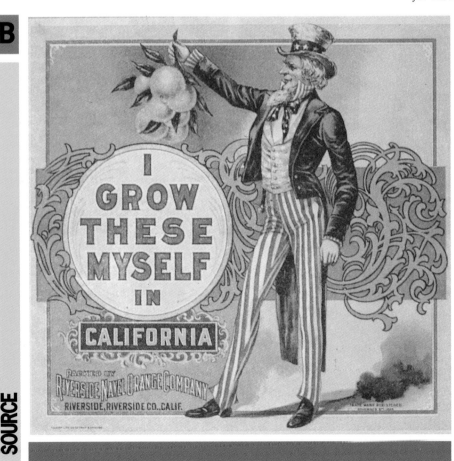

An orange box label dated about 1898.

C SOURCE

British farm labourers loading fresh strawberries onto a train bound for London in 1906.

Farmers had to adapt. Those who could switched from grain to vegetables, fruit, flowers or dairy produce. These did not suffer so badly from foreign competition. The railways were a help. For the first time, farmers could get fresh flowers, eggs, butter and fruit to the large towns quickly. Even farmers producing meat had some hope. They could buy the cheap imported grain to feed to their livestock. If they could get their beef, lamb and chicken to market fresh, they had an advantage over the imported frozen or canned meat. Some farmers were therefore able to survive. Even so, about 300,000 farm labourers had lost their jobs by 1900. Britain now produced only one third of her food and the century ended less happily for farmers than it had begun.

Arch

Joseph Arch (1826–1919) founded the National Agricultural Labourers' Union in 1872. This was a difficult time for farm labourers. Farmers were using more machines to do farm work. They were keeping more cattle and sheep, which needed fewer workers than arable farms. This caused unemployment and low wages. Joseph Arch was a Methodist preacher, a forceful speaker who urged farm workers to press for better working conditions and higher wages. For a time, the union had 100,000 members. Arch also campaigned for the vote for workers and he became MP for Norfolk in 1888.

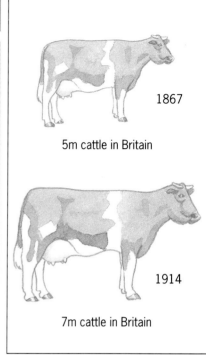

D

1867
5m cattle in Britain

1914
7m cattle in Britain

1867
1.4 hectares of wheat in Britain

1914
0.7 hectares of wheat in Britain

SOURCE

Changes in agricultural output.

2.4 Power

Horses were still by far the most common form of power used in Britain in 1750. They were used to pull, lift and carry things too heavy for men. Coalmines used horses to power the winding gear which lifted the coal out of the shafts (see Source A). Wind and water were also used to generate power. Waterwheels and windmills turned the millstones that ground corn into flour, for example. But there were problems with these sorts of power. Horses had limited strength and energy. Wind and water were not reliable (see Source B). Water power required fast-flowing streams, which only existed in some parts of the country.

A SOURCE

A painting by Paul Sandby of a coalmine in about 1786. A horse powered gin is being used to lift the coal.

B SOURCE

May 29. Another very warm day, and the dry weather is much against us as the river Ribble is very low; in the afternoons our looms go very slow for want of water. August 28. There were 30 mills stopped in Blackburn this month for want of water, and will not start again until wet weather sets in.

An extract from a Lancashire weaver's diary.

C SOURCE

The watermill at Rossett, Clwyd.

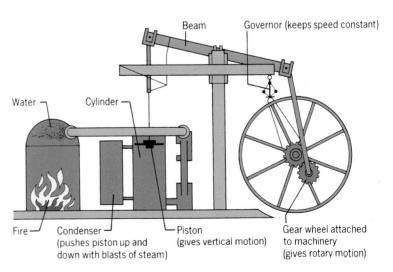

Beam

Governor (keeps speed constant)

Water

Cylinder

Fire

Condenser
(pushes piston up and
down with blasts of steam)

Piston
(gives vertical motion)

Gear wheel attached
to machinery
(gives rotary motion)

A diagram to explain the Boulton and Watt steam engine, pictured on the opposite page.

Watt

James Watt (1736–1819) has been called the inventor of the steam engine. Generations of pupils were told that he got the idea while watching a kettle boil.

Nothing could be further from the truth. Savery and Newcomen had designed steam engines before Watt. He worked to make a precision machine which used less coal and could create rotary motion.

Steam was another source of power. In 1698, **Thomas Savery** had invented a steam engine to pump out the water that flooded tin mines in Cornwall. In 1712, **Thomas Newcomen** made an improved version. There were about 300 of these engines in use by 1800. But they used lots of coal and only produced vertical motion, driving something up and down. They could not be used to power machines needing rotary motion, where things were driven round and round.

These problems were solved by **James Watt**. In 1763, he decided that he could improve Newcomen's engine. As he had no money to test his improvements, he was helped by Dr John Roebuck, the owner of the Carron Ironworks in Scotland. But in 1773, Roebuck went bankrupt. Watt's invention seemed lost. Then **Matthew Boulton**, a factory owner from Birmingham, who had heard of Watt's ideas, offered to become his partner. Watt went to work, using the engineering skills of William Murdoch, Boulton's foreman, to help him put his ideas into practice. At one stage, they couldn't make a good enough cylinder for the steam-driven piston. They were rescued by the skill of John Wilkinson, a well-known ironmaster, who made one for them. Eventually, Watt and Boulton produced a new steam engine. It was much better than Newcomen's and it could drive rotary motion (see Source D). Steam engines could now be used for all kinds of work. They made cheap mass production possible. They were at the heart of the changes in industry we call the **Industrial Revolution**. The next few units explain these changes.

SOURCE D *A steam engine designed in 1788 by James Watt.*

2.5 Textiles

In 1750, woollen cloth was Britain's most important product. The **woollen industry** was spread as widely as East Anglia, the south west of England, Yorkshire and Scotland. The raw wool was first spun into yarn on a spinning wheel; then this yarn was woven into cloth on a loom. Workers usually did the spinning and weaving in their own cottages. This was called the **domestic system**. But the growing population created more demand for clothes. This promised profits for anyone who could produce large amounts of cheap cloth. New machines were invented which enabled large amounts of cheap cloth to be produced. The Lanacashire **cotton industry** was first to use these new machines. Cotton yarn was stronger than wool and more suited to the machines. Cotton cloth was also more comfortable to wear.

Spinning wool before the Industrial Revolution.

In 1733, **John Kay** invented the **flying shuttle**. It was a device added to the hand-loom to speed up weaving. This was followed in 1765, by the **spinning jenny**, invented by **James Hargreaves**. This machine could spin six threads of yarn at once. Both of these machines could be used in the workers' cottages. By 1788, there were 20,000 spinning jennies in use and the cotton industry was booming.

More change was to come. In 1769, **Richard Arkwright** patented the **water frame**. This machine for spinning yarn was powered by a water wheel. In 1779, **Samuel Crompton** made an even better machine called the **mule**.

It was many years before an efficient weaving machine was made. Then **Edmund Cartwright** invented a **power loom** in 1785. It was not widely used until it was improved by William Horrocks in 1803.

These machines were too large for workers' cottages. They needed a water wheel or a steam engine to power them. The new machines were housed in **mills** or **factories**. Women and children could look after the machines; there was less work for men. Mills first became concentrated in areas of the country

At Hyde are two factories, sited between a torrent which supplies the engines with water and two coalmines which supply fuel. Mr Ashton employs 1500 workpeople of both sexes. One immense room, filled with looms, contains 400 of them. The houses lived in by the workers form long and large streets. Mr Ashton has built three hundred houses which he lets at 3s (15p) per week.

An extract from a report written in about 1840.

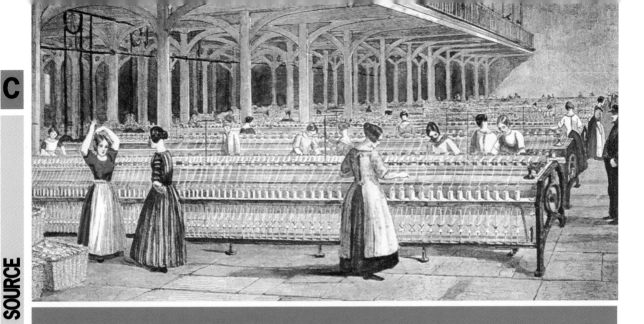

Cotton spinning during the Industrial Revolution.

close to fast-flowing streams and later near sources of cheap coal for the steam engines. By 1830, 80% of cotton spinning was steam powered and there were 100,000 steam-powered machines for spinning. The woollen industry also changed, but it lagged about 30 years behind.

The changes in **textiles** are typical of the Industrial Revolution. They made cotton a vital part of the economy in Britain. By 1850, about 350,000 people worked in the cotton industry. About 200,000 were women and 15,000 children. Another 200,000 worked in woollens. Cotton provided 35% of British exports and remained the biggest export product until the Second World War.

Arkwright

Richard Arkwright (1732–92) began his working life as an apprentice barber. He ended up owning factories worth about £800,000. His success came from his 'water frame'. By the 1760s, new inventions meant that cotton weavers could work much faster than spinners.

Arkwright improved a spinning machine invented by Lewis Paul in the 1730s. It was driven by water power and spun strong cotton yarn extremely fast, on long spindles. He built factories full of water frames in Lancashire and Derbyshire. They earned him wealth, fame and a knighthood.

The Cloth Hall, Leeds, in 1813. Wealthy merchants at work. Yorkshire became the centre of the woollen industry. First its fast flowing Pennine streams and later the nearby coalfields provided cheap power for the mills. Hull became the chief port for its exports.

2.6 Iron and Steel

In 1750 Britain's iron industry was still very small. It was sited mainly in Shropshire, near sources of iron ore and supplies of timber which provided the charcoal used as fuel in the furnaces. Several inventions brought major changes in the iron industry.

Charcoal was becoming scarce and expensive. In 1709, **Abraham Darby** began using **coke** instead of charcoal to make **pig iron** at his ironworks at **Coalbrookdale** in Shropshire. Slowly others copied his methods. This meant that ironworks were not tied to woodland. Areas which had iron ore and coal deposits started to make cheap **pig iron**.

However, this pig iron was only suitable for making cast iron. By 1784, **Henry Cort** was using a new method for turning the pig iron into **wrought iron**. He reheated the pig iron in a **forge**, then 'puddled' or stirred it to remove most of the impurities. After it cooled, he passed the metal through grooved rollers which removed the rest of the impurities. This **puddling and rolling** made it possible to produce wrought iron quickly and cheaply.

In 1828, **James Neilson** made ironmaking even cheaper by reducing the amount of fuel needed. He did this by making the bellows pump hot air into the furnaces, not cold. This improvement was only used in Scotland for a while and it gave the iron industry there a boost (see Source B). In 1840, **James Nasmyth** produced a steam-powered hammer which made forging much quicker and easier.

The ironmasters were keen to show how useful iron could be. Abraham Darby's grandson (Abraham Darby III), built a famous iron bridge across the River Severn. John 'iron-mad' Wilkinson was even buried in a metal coffin. It was now possible to build the tools, machines, bridges, and railways of the Industrial Revolution (see Source C). Ironmaking became one of Britain's most important industries. British iron production in 1750 was about 30,000 tons; by 1830, it was 1 million tons; by 1870, 6 million tons.

Steel remained very expensive to make until after 1850. Britain's total output was still only 60,000 tons.

Making iron and steel in 1750

Iron ore was melted in a furnace which was fired with charcoal. When the molten iron cooled it became **pig iron.** Some of the molten iron was poured directly into moulds to make pots, pans and pipes. This was **cast iron;** it was impure and brittle. Impurities could be removed by reheating and hammering the pig iron in the forge. This made a tough pliable metal called **wrought iron;** it was used to make nails and chains. **Steel** is a hard and flexible metal made from molten pig iron with carbon and manganese added.

SOURCE

A painting from 1772 by Joseph Wright showing a forge. The red hot pig iron is being held on an anvil under a trip hammer. These were driven by water wheels and later by steam engines.

But in 1856, **Henry Bessemer** invented a **'converter'** which blasted oxygen through molten pig iron to remove impurities. Then carefully-measured carbon and manganese could be added to make steel. Bessemer set up a steel works in Sheffield in 1858. In 1867, **William Siemens** invented a new way of making steel, the **open hearth** method. But neither method worked well with British iron ore, which contained too much phosphorus. Britain relied on imported ore. By 1880, British steel production reached 2 million tons. But German and American steelmaking grew faster.

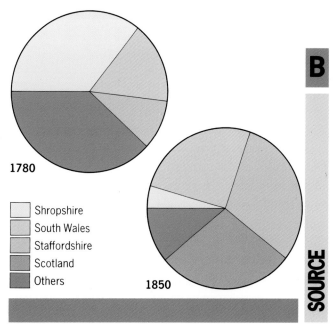

B SOURCE

1780

- Shropshire
- South Wales
- Staffordshire
- Scotland
- Others

1850

The location of British iron production.

Wilkinson

John Wilkinson (1728–1808) was an ironmaster. In 1774, he invented a lathe for boring the barrels of cannons and made a fortune during the Seven Years War (1756–63). He later used the same machine to make cylinders for James Watt's steam engines. He had a gift for applying ideas. He was one of the first to use coke smelting; he used a steam engine to power his trip hammers. He was a great salesman for iron goods. He became known as 'iron mad Wilkinson'. He helped Abraham Darby build the first iron bridge in 1770 and built a cast iron chapel for his Methodist friends. He built the first ever iron barge in 1787 and, in the same year, sent 40 miles of iron pipes for Paris's water supply. When he died, he was buried in an iron coffin.

C SOURCE

Since cast iron has got all the rage,
And scarcely a thing's made
    without it,
As I live in this cast iron age,
I mean to say something about it.
We have cast iron fenders and
    grates,
We have cast iron pokers and
    tongs sir,
And soon we'll have cast iron
    plates,
And cast iron small clothes ere
    long sir.

Extracts from a popular ballad from the 1820s.

D SOURCE

'Forging the Shaft', a painting dated 1877. The steam hammers had not taken all of the heavy work out of the forging process.

2.7 Coal

In 1750, coalmining was a small, but important industry. It was centred in the north east of England and produced about **5 million tons** per year, mainly to heat people's homes. After 1750 the demand for coal increased. There were more homes to heat, and steam engines and the iron industry used coal for fuel. Later, railways used coal too. This growing demand promised big profits. Landowners were willing to invest their money to mine deeper and deeper in search of coal. But deeper mining meant more technical problems.

Water caused **flooding** in the mines. Pumps driven by the **steam engines** of Newcomen, Savery and Watt were the solution here. By 1775, there were 400 steam driven pumps on coalfields. But **ventilation** was a more difficult problem. Gases seeped out of the coal deposits. Some suffocated the miners; others exploded on contact with the flames which were the miners' only source of light. To remove these gases, deep mines were given two shafts. A **furnace** at the bottom of one heated the air. As the hot air rose it pulled fresh air down the other shaft. This fresh air was circulated underground by opening and closing **trap doors**. In 1815, Sir Humphrey Davy invented a **safety lamp**. A flame burned in the lamp behind a wire gauze which prevented contact with the explosive gas. Later, **steam-powered fans** were used to blow fresh air into the mines, but these were not common until after 1860.

B The down-cast shaft is called the John Pit. It is 204 yards deep and has a steam engine for drawing the coal and a horse gin for lifting the men when the machine is crippled. The air furnace shaft is called the William Pitt. It has only a horse gin. Trap doors, attended by boys about 8 years old, are placed to divert the air through proper channels. The air is accelerated through the workings by a large fire in this up-cast shaft.

A description of the Felling Colliery in Durham.

The pithead of a coalmine. Horses and mules are still being used for transport. But there is a steam-powered water pump in the centre of the painting and steam-powered winding gear on the left.

Lifting and carrying the coal was the third major problem. **Horses** were kept underground and used for pulling coal wagons along the shafts. Workers – often women – were used to carry the coal in baskets up ladders to the surface. **Horse gins** were used as lifting gear at the pithead. However, steam power brought improvements. From 1800 steam engines were used to wind cages carrying the miners or the coal up the shafts. **Wire ropes**, invented in 1834 and made from wrought iron, made this much safer. **Steam-powered wagon ways** carried coal around the pithead at some mines from about 1810; later, **trains** carried coal cheaply to all parts of Britain.

The coalfields of Britain in about 1800.

Central Scotland

North East

Yorkshire, Derbyshire, Notts.

South Wales

Midlands

By 1900, 'King Coal' was a major industry, spread over many parts of Britain. It produced nearly **200 million tons** per year and employed over one million people. About a quarter of the coal produced was exported. The rest provided fuel for industry and heat for the growing population.

Davy

Sir Humphrey Davy (1778–1824) invented a safety lamp in 1815, which could light the mines without setting off explosive gases like 'fire damp' (methane).

Before Davy's invention, mines employed a **fireman**. He went into the mine first, dressed in wet sacking and lying in a hollow covered by planks, pulling a lighted candle on a string through the mineshaft. This set off any pockets of gas before the men started to work, using lighted candles to see by. There were many accidents with this system. Generations of miners were grateful for Davy lamps.

C

A Yorkshire miner. A locomotive designed by John Blenkinsop is working on the steam-powered wagon way behind him.

2.8 An Entrepreneur – Josiah Wedgwood

In 1750 most people used pewter mugs and plates. Crockery was heavy and uneven in shape and colour. The wealthy used imported fine china. But tea and coffee drinking was growing. The middle classes began to demand china. This made the Staffordshire potteries grow, and made Josiah Wedgwood famous.

In 1759 Wedgwood set up his own pottery, mixing china clay from Cornwall and ground up flint to make smooth china called **creamware**. He experimented, writing discoveries in code to keep them secret. He learned to add kaolin to glaze to stop it cracking and to make more consistent colours. He developed new products, **black basalt** in 1769 and **jasperware** in 1773. Wedgwood also invented a **pyrometer**, a thermometer for the kilns, and used lathes and a steam engine at his works.

He also publicized his goods. He used travelling salesmen. He gave back money to dissatisfied customers and replaced goods broken in transit. Wedgwood sent samples to the royal Court. After he sold creamware to the Queen in 1765, he changed the name of his creamware to **queensware** and took the title of 'Potter to the Queen'. Wedgwood pottery was now fashionable; sales boomed. In 1773 he sold a 952 piece dinner service to Empress Catherine the Great of Russia. Sales abroad grew. Wedgwood used high class **ornamental ware**, such as vases, to create his image. People at the time admired classical Greece and Rome; Wedgwood's queensware, black basalt and jasper were ideal for this neoclassical art. He used the finest artists of the day to decorate his ornamental ware. This made his reputation. But his main sales were **useful ware**, plates, cups, and teapots.

Wedgwood ran an efficient business. He used a Liverpool merchant, Thomas Bentley, as his partner to look after sales. He helped to fund new roads and the Grand Trunk Canal to cut transport costs and breakages. In 1769, he spent £3000 on a new factory, **Etruria**, on the canal bank. He divided the production of pottery into stages and made his craftsmen concentrate on one stage each, to improve their speed and skill.

Wedgwood mixed marketing and business sense with science and art. Other potters were also successful; but none matched Wedgwood. He turned a local craft into a national industry.

A blue jasperware trinket box showing neoclassical design; part of Wedgwood's ornamental ware.

Wedgwood's London showroom for ornamental and useful ware, 1809.

Our black ware blisters with a rough pinholy surface. The causes appear to be the manganese not being washed sufficiently and the ware having too hot a fire. (**1793**)

I have just had the honour of the Duke of Marlborough, Lord Gower, Lord Spencer and others at my works. They have bought some things. (**1765**)

My reason for wanting a large room was to show various table and dessert services completely set out. These articles may every few days be so altered as to render a whole new scene. (**1767**)

The Great People have had these vases in their palaces long enough for them to be seen and admired by the middling class, which is vastly superior in number. The character of the vases is established and the middling people will probably buy quantities of them at a reduced price.(**1771**)

You will see the importance in most manufactures of making the greatest quantity possible in a given time. Rent goes on whether we make much or little. Wages to some workers is nearly the same whether we make 20 dozen or 10 dozen vases per week. (**1771**)

Extracts from the letters of Josiah Wedgwood (See also Unit 2.11, Source D).

Josiah Wedgwood

Wedgwood was born into a family of potters at Burslem in Staffordshire on 12 July 1730. He was an apprentice potter under his brother, Thomas.

As a boy he fell ill with smallpox and nearly died. He spent months in bed and developed a love for reading. Later in life, he fell from his horse, injuring his leg so badly it had to be amputated.

When he built his factory at Etruria, he also built houses for his workers and their families. He died in 1795.

2.9 The Industrial Peak?

By the middle of the 19th century, Britain was known as the **'Workshop of the World'**. Some people's jobs, like shopkeepers and domestic servants, remained unchanged. But steam-powered, coal-fuelled, mechanized mass-production had changed many jobs. Britain had one quarter of the world's international trade. The country basked in confidence.

In 1851, Britain staged the **Great Exhibition** to celebrate the achievements of British and foreign industry. A magnificent exhibition building, over 500 metres long and 125 metres wide and made of iron and glass, was erected in Hyde Park. It was called the **Crystal Palace**. It was open for over five months, included 7,000 British exhibitors and 6,000 from abroad and was visited by over six million people. Railway companies brought trainloads from all over the country. The exhibition cost £300,000 to set up, but made a profit of £186,000. This money was used to build the Royal Albert Hall, the Science Museum, the Natural History Museum and the Victoria and Albert Museum.

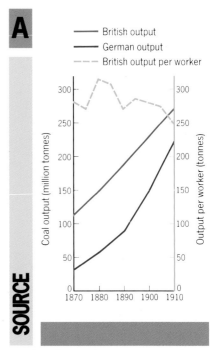

A SOURCE

Coal production between 1870 and 1910.

B SOURCE

A mural painting called 'Iron and Steel'. It was painted in 1861 by William Bell Scott at Wallington Hall in Northumberland.

A machine hall at the Great Exhibition of 1851.

Britain's people benefited from this prosperity. Wages generally rose while prices fell. Consumption of meat, tea, sugar and beer all rose. Many famous retail companies like Cadburys, Boots and Liptons started at this time.

But even at the height of Britain's industrial success, there were danger signs. **Foreign competition** was growing. American and Australian farmers were producing large quanties of grain and meat. Iron and coal industries began to develop in Germany and the United States. Textile industries began to grow in developing countries like India. **Steam cargo ships** brought their goods cheaply to Britain.

These competitors often used **new methods** while the British stayed loyal to the older ones which had been successful for them in the past. Foreign companies adopted electric power; British factories kept steam. Some foreign ironmasters used open hearth, then electric arc furnaces; many British ones kept the Bessemer process. Foreign textile producers used automatic looms; the British kept their mules. The new industries of 1900, for example, chemicals and dyes, developed abroad, not in Britain. The Americans, French and Germans excelled at developing motor cars, while Britain remained the leading producer of trains. By the end of the 19th century, Britain was losing its place as the 'Workshop of the World'.

Lipton

Sir Thomas Lipton (1850–1931) emigrated to the US in 1865. He worked on tobacco and rice plantations and in a grocer's shop. In 1870, he returned to Glasgow to open a grocer's store of his own; he soon had many more. He was a millionaire by the age of 30. He also ran tea and rubber plantations. Lipton's tea is still famous today. Thomas Lipton was also a keen sailor and tried four times, without success, to win the Americas Cup.

D Year by year the smoke curling from the chimneys of Indian cotton mills increases in volume. It writes the doom of Lancashire.

From an article called 'The Peril of Lancashire' in 'The London Magazine', 1913.

E American ingenuity has undoubtedly taken the lead in making motors of all kinds.

S. S. Wheeler, writing in the 'Illustrated London News' in 1888.

2.10 Transport – Roads

Many of the products of the Industrial Revolution were **heavy** and **bulky**. Grain, wool, iron and coal are examples. Such goods are **difficult** and **expensive** to transport. Other goods, like meat or milk, needed **fast** transport to get them to market while they were still fresh. For all of these reasons, transport was very important during the Industrial Revolution.

In 1750, most people and goods were transported by road on horses, packhorses, carts or stagecoaches. But the roads were in very poor condition. Outside towns, they were usually just tracks created by frequent use. They were muddy in winter and deeply rutted in summer. Since 1555, the law had said that the rich people in each parish had to pay for tools and materials to repair the roads; poorer people had to do six days unpaid work per year on them. But this system did not work.

As the demand for better transport grew, some people saw potential profit in building better roads. They set up groups, called **turnpike trusts**, to run stretches of road like a business. Acts of Parliament gave them permission to charge **tolls** (fees) to all the travellers who used certain roads. In return, they would use some of these fees to pay for improvements to the road. They employed expert road builders to repair or replace the old roads. The most famous road-builders were **John Metcalfe**, **Thomas Telford** and **John Macadam**.

A SOURCE

I left Tonbridge and came to Lewes through the deepest, dirtiest roads in all that part of England. Sometimes a whole summer is not dry enough to make the roads passable. Here I saw a lady drawn to church in her coach by six oxen, the road being so deep and stiff that no horses could go in it.

From 'A Tour Through the Whole Island of Great Britain' (1724) by Daniel Defoe.

This is a scene from a country market town during the coaching era, recorded by Thomas Rowlandson. Note the wide range of road users.

B SOURCE

A crowded stagecoach reaches a toll house. A painting dated 1829.

The road from Salisbury to Romsey is without exception the finest I ever saw. The trustees of that road deserve all the praise that can be given. It is everywhere broad enough for 3 carriages to pass. Lying in straight lines, with an edge of grass the whole way, it has more the appearance of an elegant gravel walk than a high road.

Arthur Young, commenting on the roads in southern England during his tour of 1768.

Macadam

John Loudon Macadam (1756–1836) was the surveyor of the Bristol Turnpike Trust, caring for the roads in the area. These roads were very busy, and quickly developed potholes. Macadam became famous for finding a cheap way to repair them.

He used gangs of unskilled labourers to break stones into tiny pieces; these were raked and pounded into the potholes. Coach and wagon wheels then crushed the tiny stones into a smooth, solid mass. His road surfaces became so popular that he worked for 107 trusts, repairing 200 miles of road.

In modern times, macadamized roads are bound together with tar and the surface is called tarmacadam – tarmac for short.

Merchants were glad to pay small fees in exchange for better roads. Stagecoach companies also used them. They could offer much better services on the turnpikes. A journey from London to York took five days in 1750; by 1840 it took only one day. Coaching inns sprang up along the routes to provide food and fresh horses. From 1784, the stagecoaches carried the **Royal Mail**. By 1840, 23,000 people were employed by the turnpike trusts and over 30,000 by the coaching companies.

Eight turnpike trusts were set up between 1700 and 1750 and 55 between 1750 and 1800. By 1830, there were 1,000 turnpike trusts, controlling 23,000 miles of road, about one sixth of the total roads in Britain. But the 'golden age of coaching' came to an end in the 1840s. The next two units explain how canals and railways took the place of long-distance road transport.

2.11 *T*ransport – Canals

Because Britain is an island, a great deal of trade had always been sent by boat along the coasts. Coal from north east England usually came to London by sea. From the ports, barges took goods to inland areas along rivers. Water transport was quicker than road and boats could take heavier loads. But rivers had disadvantages. They meandered and in some places were too shallow for boats to pass. There were many river improvement schemes before 1750. But still rivers flooded in winter and bridges and fords blocked river traffic. Some important industrial areas, such as Birmingham and the Potteries (in Staffordshire) did not have navigable rivers.

In 1757, the **Sankey Brook Canal** was opened. It linked the coalfields around St. Helens to the River Mersey and supplied the people and manufacturers of Liverpool with coal. It was paid for by local businessmen. In 1764, the **Bridgewater Canal**, from Worsley to Manchester, was built by **James Brindley**. The cost of this 10 mile canal was £200,000, paid by the **Duke of Bridgewater**. He owned a coal mine at Worsley and wanted to reduce the cost of taking his coal to Manchester. In 1765, he halved the price of his coal and still made a profit. The Duke also charged other traders to use the canal. He was soon making £80,000 per year in fees.

Other businessmen employed engineers like **James Brindley**, **Thomas Telford** and **William Jessop** to build canals. To raise the money, they set up companies to build the canals, and sold shares in the companies. Shares in the Birmingham Canal Company were first issued at £140 each. The canal was so profitable that its shares sold at £1,170 by 1792.

The main canals and navigable rivers of Britain in 1830.

A SOURCE

It will mean a great increase in trade to the trading towns of the North if goods can be sent by water. At this time, to get goods to Rawcliffe they are sent 22 miles by land. This is expensive and many times the goods receive damage through the badness of the roads.

Part of a letter from the cloth merchants of Wakefield arguing for improvements to the River Calder in about 1700.

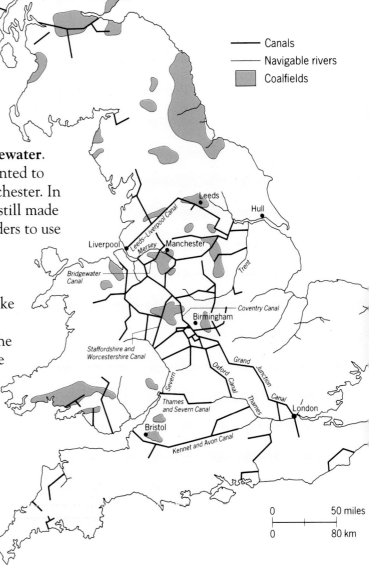

Canals
Navigable rivers
Coalfields

Leeds
Hull
Leeds–Liverpool Canal
Liverpool
Mersey
Manchester
Bridgewater Canal
Trent
Coventry Canal
Birmingham
Staffordshire and Worcestershire Canal
Severn
Oxford Canal
Grand Junction Canal
Thames and Severn Canal
Thames
London
Bristol
Kennet and Avon Canal

0 ———— 50 miles
0 ———— 80 km

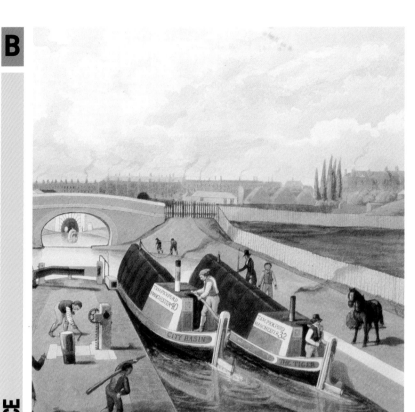

A view of the Regent's Canal at the entrance to Islington Tunnel in 1827. Canals brought grain from the countryside to London and carried its imports from abroad inland.

A good horse on a level railed wagon way can draw only about eight tons, whereas on a canal in a well constructed iron boat it can draw 65 tons in addition to the boat.

A letter to a magazine in 1810. On the roads, it took four horses to carry one ton.

The price of carriage of clay and flint for pottery in Staffordshire, which is 15*s*. (shillings) per ton, will be reduced to 2*s*. The carriage of the earthenware in return will be reduced from 28*s*. to about 12*s*. per ton, which must greatly increase the export of that manufacture.

Josiah Wedgwood, commenting on plans for a canal to link the Rivers Trent and Mersey in 1765. (One shilling = 5p).

Brindley's most famous canal is the **Grand Trunk Canal**, which links the Rivers Trent and Mersey and runs through the Potteries. It was finished in 1777. By 1790, a canal network linked the four major ports of Bristol, Liverpool, Hull and London. Enthusiasm continued. In the 1790s a further 50 canals were built. Some of these were in rural areas and never made great profits for their owners, even though they did bring benefits to the people who lived near them.

The canals provided cheap, reliable transport in the vital early stages of the Industrial Revolution. This was just as important in getting raw materials and fuel to manufacturers and farmers as it was for getting their goods to market. The canals were also useful for transporting breakable goods, like pottery. By 1830, about 40,000 workers were employed on the canals. But by the 1840s the canals were in decline. They had been overtaken by a faster and cheaper form of transport – the railways.

Brindley

James Brindley (1716–72) was an engineer who became Britain's most famous canal builder. He could hardly read or write but was a great solver of problems. For the Bridgewater Canal, he built a huge aqueduct to carry the canal over the River Irwell. He also taught his navvies (canal workmen) to mix clay, sand and water to make a sticky lining for his canals, to stop the water from seeping away.

2.12 Transport – Railways

In 1750 wagon ways were common in the coalfields. They used horses to pull carts of coal along metal tracks. In 1804, **Richard Trevithick** built a **locomotive**, a steam engine which could pull carts along rails. This was the first railway engine. But it was unreliable; he only built it to demonstrate on a circular track. Others soon followed with improved versions. **William Hedley** built the '**Puffing Billy**' in 1813 to use on the wagon ways of Wylam Colliery. By 1823, there were 20 locomotives moving coal on wagon ways.

Mineowners in Durham decided to build a railed track to take their coal 25 miles from **Stockton to Darlington**. They employed **George Stephenson** to build it. He persuaded them to let him use steam locomotives. In 1825, the line was opened. It took two engines, 'Locomotive No 1' and 'Experiment' to pull 21 coal wagons at eight miles per hour. The railway was soon making a profit. In 1830, Stephenson built another steam railway from **Liverpool to Manchester**. At first, the owners were not sure whether to use horses, locomotives or stationary steam engines pulling carts along with chains. They held the **Rainhill Trials** as a test to help them decide. Stephenson's locomotive the '**Rocket**' won the competition with a speed of 15 miles per hour. When the line opened its trains ran at 40 miles per hour. It was intended to carry trade to and from the port. But by 1850, it was also carrying up to 200,000 passengers per week.

A

SOURCE

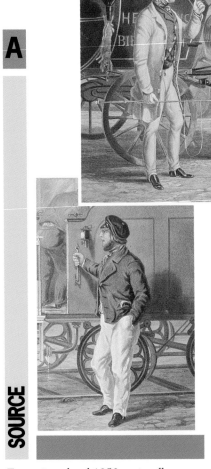

Engravings dated 1852, pointedly entitled 'Contrasts – The Driver of 1832 and the Driver of 1852'.

B

Farmers found railways as useful as manufacturers.

SOURCE

'The Railway Station' by William Frith, 1862.

There were soon so many proposals for new lines that people called it '**railway mania**'. Over 50 schemes were approved by Parliament between 1825 and 1835; in 1836 and 1837, 39 new lines were agreed; and in 1846 alone a further 5,000 miles were started. By 1900, Britain had 22,000 miles of track.

The railways helped **industry** with cheaper carriage of raw materials and finished products. Manufacturers could sell cheaper goods and still make more profit. Railways also bought from industry – iron for rails and locomotives, coal for fuel and bricks for embankments and stations.

Farmers not only got their produce to market cheaper, they could send it further and quicker. This was important for perishable produce like milk and fruit and flowers.

The railways also provided **jobs**. It took 20,000 workers to build the London to Birmingham line. In 1854, there were 90,000 jobs in railway maintenance. Whole new **towns** emerged. Crewe grew from a place with 203 people in 1841 to a railway depot and town with a population of 18,000 in 1871.

As well as cheaper food and goods and more work, there were other public benefits. The mail speeded up; national newspapers flourished; travel became easier. Holidays to seaside towns like Brighton became possible.

At first many people opposed the railways. The coaching and canal companies could not compete with the speed of rail. Some people complained about the pollution; others said that sparks from the engines would burn their crops and the noise would upset farm animals. Some towns, like Northampton and Oxford, refused to let the railways in for several years. But eventually the railways were accepted everywhere. Britain built the world's first rail network and it became a pillar of Britain's success in the mid 19th century.

Stephenson

George Stephenson (1781–1848) is sometimes called 'the father of the railways'. He did not invent the locomotive, but he made 16 of them, and many miles of track; this got businessmen to support the railways. In 1830, crowds came to the opening of his Liverpool to Manchester line. One incident marred the success of the day. To get government support, a minister, William Huskisson, was invited. He stepped in the way of a train and became the world's first railway fatality.

2.13 Transport – Britain Overtaken

Many new methods of transport, apart from railways, developed in the 19th century. Britain did not dominate these. Some were lasting, like **bicycles** and **trams**. Others were less practical, like long-distance balloons and steam-powered cars. The two main developments were in **shipping** and **motor cars**.

In 1845, a new **sailing ship** appeared. It was the American '**Rainbow**', the first **clipper**. Clippers were designed to cross the oceans of the world at record speed. Britain's best known clipper was the **Cutty Sark**. Most clippers were American.

Then came **steam-powered ships**. In Scotland, William Symington built a steam-powered riverboat called the '**Charlotte Dundas**' in 1804. A steam ferry called the '**Comet**' was used to take people along the River Clyde from 1812. But it was 1838 before steamships took to the seas. In that year two steamships, the '**Sirius**', an American ship, and the '**Great Western**', a paddle steamer built by **Isambard Kingdom Brunel**, both crossed the Atlantic.

Next came **iron ships**. Brunel's '**Great Britain**' was launched in 1843. In 1881, the '**Servia**' became the world's first ocean-going **steel ship**. It was built in Scotland and could carry 1,250 passengers. Brunel's '**Great Eastern**' was even bigger. It could carry 4,000 passengers. This was the era of the ocean-going passenger liners, dominated by two British companies: the **Cunard Line** and **P and O Line**.

B SOURCE

SMALLEST & SHARPEST CLIPPER LOADIN
Coleman's California Line
FOR SAN FRANCISCO

The A 1 Extreme Clipper Ship
SYREN
GREEN, Commander, is now rapidly Loading at PIER 11, E. R.
This beautiful little Clipper has made some of the fastest passages on reco
From SAN FRANCISCO to BOSTON, in 100 DAYS,
From NEW-YORK to SAN FRANCISCO, in 120 DAYS,
From CALCUTTA to BOSTON, in 96 DAYS,
always delivering her cargoes IN PERFECT ORDER. Shippers will find
the MOST DESIRABLE VESSEL NOW LOADING. For balance of Freight, apply to
WM. T. COLEMAN & CO., 161 Pearl Street,
Agents at San Francisco, Messrs. W. T. Coleman & Co. Near W

A poster, dated about 1850, advertising the American clipper, 'The Syren'.

C SOURCE

The forests of North America gave the Americans a great advantage in the building of wooden ships. Their huge trade in cotton, timber and grain gave them plenty of business.

From 'Transport 1750–1980' by Simon Mason, 1985.

A SOURCE

'Red Jacket', an American clipper pictured in about 1850.

D **SOURCE**

The luxury P and O liner, 'S.S. Ophir' at Port Said in about 1900.

In 1862, **Etienne Lenoir**, a French engineer, produced a car with a **gas-powered** engine that could run at three miles per hour on roads. It was never a commercial success, but it was the first step towards the mass production of motor cars. Improved versions were developed by **Siegfried Markus**, an Austrian, in 1868, and by **Nikolaus Otto**, a German, in 1876. In 1883, **Gottlieb Daimler**, a manager at Otto's factory, made a **petrol** engine which could be fitted to a car or a bicycle. **Karl Benz**, another German, also produced a motorbike, this one with three wheels, in 1884. By 1885, Benz was selling petrol-driven motor cars. The first British motor car was produced in 1896 by Fred Lanchester. **Rolls-Royce** began manufacturing in 1906. By 1903, there were almost 20,000 cars in Britain, but most of them were foreign.

F **SOURCE**

The major steps forward in the petrol engine were all made on the continent. Work in this country was hampered by laws passed under pressure from the horse and railway interests to keep steam carriages (cars) off the roads.

From 'An Economic and Social History of Great Britain, 1760–1970' by Trevor May, 1987. (One law passed in Britain in 1865 said that all motorized vehicles on the roads had to keep below four mph and be preceded by a man walking along with a red flag to warn other roadusers).

Rolls-Royce

Sir Frederick Henry Royce, born in 1863, was a Manchester engineer who started to build cars in 1904.

Charles Stewart Rolls was born in 1877. He was a car dealer, who went into business with Royce in 1906 to form the world famous Rolls-Royce Ltd.

Both men were fascinated by aeroplanes. In 1910, Rolls became the first man to fly non-stop across the Channel and back. Royce lived until 1933 and developed aeroplane engines like the Merlin, which was later used in Spitfires.

E **SOURCE**

De Dion car factory, France, c. 1898.

2.14 An Engineer – I.K. Brunel

Isambard Kingdom Brunel was born in 1806. As a young man he helped his father, Marc Brunel, to design a tunnel under the Thames. He later designed the **Clifton suspension bridge** over the river Avon at Bristol and docks at Bristol and Plymouth. But his greatest works were in railways and steam shipping.

In 1833, at the age of 24, he was employed to build the **Great Western Railway**, from London to Bristol. The line was started in 1835. It took six years and £6.5 million to build. The biggest challenge was the **Box Tunnel** near Bath which took over two years, 30 million bricks and a ton of gunpowder every week to build. Accidents claimed 100 lives during its construction. The Great Western Railway also boasted huge buildings at **Bristol Temple Meads** and **Paddington Station** in London. Brunel used rails 7ft apart instead of 4ft 8½ins as in the rest of the country. This **broad gauge** gave a safer and more comfortable ride at above 50 miles per hour. But different gauges made it impossible for the same trains to travel all over the country. Eventually, Parliament insisted on a standard gauge of 4ft 8½ins.

Brunel then turned to the design of ships. In 1838 he launched the **Great Western**, a paddle steamer with an oak hull. At 1320 tons, it was the largest steamship in the world. It crossed the Atlantic in fifteen days. In 1843, he launched his **Great Britain**. This had an iron hull and a screw propeller, stronger than paddles. It can still be seen in Bristol docks.

Isambard Kingdom Brunel.

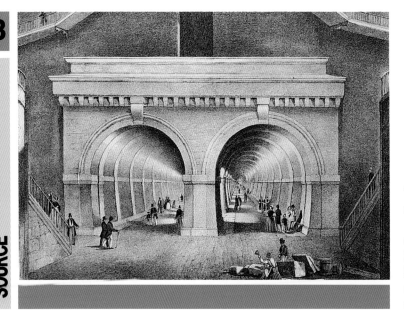

The entrance to the Rotherhithe tunnel under the River Thames, opened in 1843. The tunnel was only two metres under the river in places and water broke through several times. The tunnel had been intended for road traffic, but the Brunels ran short of money and it was eventually used only by pedestrians.

SOURCE

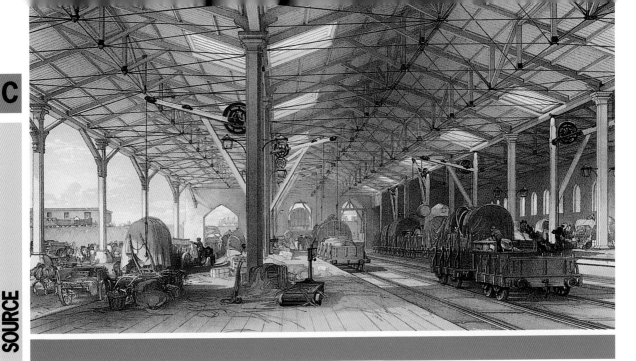

The western terminus of the Great Western Railway, Temple Meads Station at Bristol.

But his most famous ship was the **Great Eastern**. It was 20,000 tons and remained the largest ship in the world for 40 years. It had steam powered screw propellers and paddles and also carried sails. It used 300 tons of coal per day, but still had room for 5000 tons of cargo and 4,000 passengers. When it was launched in 1858, it became stuck in the mud at Millwall docks. On its maiden voyage, a boiler blew up and five people were killed. In 1866, the **Great Eastern** was used to lay the first telegraph cable to America. But commercially it was a failure. It was so big, it was difficult to fill and run profitably.

Brunel died in 1859. He left huge monuments to his engineering skills. Some schemes, like the Clifton bridge, were finished after his death. Some, like his idea for an atmospheric railway, using air suction to power trains up to 70mph without the noise and pollution of steam, remained just ideas.

Brunel

Sir Marc Isambard Brunel was I.K. Brunel's father. He was born in France in 1769, but fled to New York in 1793 to escape the violence of the French Revolution. He moved to Britain in 1799.

He was also an engineer and specialized in tunnelling. His tunnel under the Thames took from 1825 until 1842 to complete. It was 460 metres long, 11 metres wide and 7 metres high. Over a million people came to see its opening ceremony in 1843.

D

SOURCE

'The Great Eastern'.

2.15 Connections – The Industrial Revolution

Part Two of this book has looked at changes which took place in Britain after 1750 in population, farming, industry and transport. They all form part of the Industrial Revolution. One way of picturing these changes is shown below.

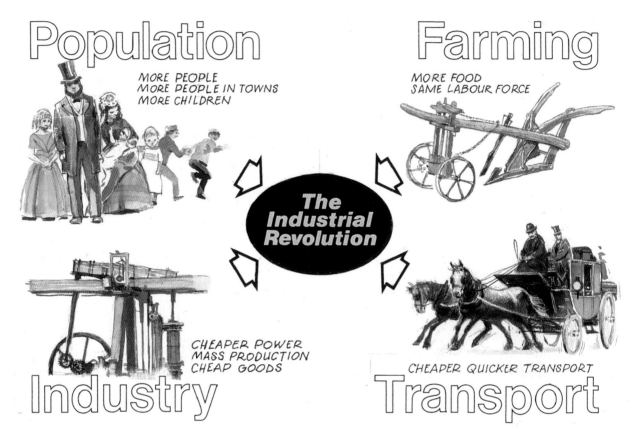

Population
MORE PEOPLE
MORE PEOPLE IN TOWNS
MORE CHILDREN

Farming
MORE FOOD
SAME LABOUR FORCE

The Industrial Revolution

Industry
CHEAPER POWER
MASS PRODUCTION
CHEAP GOODS

Transport
CHEAPER QUICKER TRANSPORT

But the diagram above is misleading. It makes the changes in population, farming, industry and transport look separate. There were, in fact, important **connections** between the changes. For example, it is possible to show connections between population increase and changes in farming. More people led to more demand for food; this caused food prices to rise, which provided profits for farmers to enclose their fields. So population increase caused farming changes. But farming changes also supported population changes. More food allowed the population to grow; without more food the extra people would have starved. So population changes and farming changes were not separate; they went hand in hand. Each change supported the other. The changes became stronger and faster. This is true of all the changes in population, farming, industry and transport.

Industrial Revolution

In many ways, the phrase Industrial Revolution is misleading.

'Revolution' makes you think about a complete and sudden change. But the Industrial Revolution was more about steady development than sudden change.

A better view of the Industrial Revolution is shown on the diagram below. All of the elements needed to bring about the Industrial Revolution are shown as a whirlwind. It shows the changes in population, farming, industry and transport. In this whirlwind, all the changes are feeding upon each other, to make Britain an industrialized country.

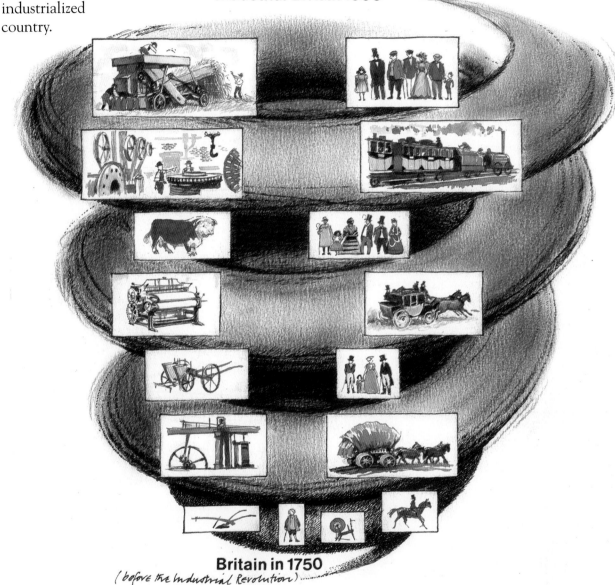

Industrial Britain 1900

Britain in 1750
(before the Industrial Revolution)

The Industrial Revolution

In a sense, the Industrial Revolution is still going on. Industry, farming and transport are still changing and these changes continue to affect our lives today.

We are also now experiencing a revolution in technology, with the development of computers, satellite television and electronic media

2.16 Life and Work in the Towns – A Study in Depth

This study looks at the harsh living and working conditions of poor people in the towns of the early 19th century. It then looks at why it took a long time for changes to be made.

The Growth of Towns

Between 1750 and 1900 the number of people living in towns of 25,000 or more grew from 20% to 70% of the population. The towns which people lived in also grew much bigger. London and the industrial towns grew fastest. For example, between 1801 and 1901, Glasgow's population grew from 75,000 to 900,000. This amount of change was bound to cause problems.

Houses were squeezed into the centres of towns or around the factories. Landlords crammed as many people into houses as they could. The **water supply** was another problem. In London's Highgate, water was bought by the bucketful from stand-pipes in the street; at Hyde, Manchester, people paid one shilling (5p) per week to buy water from carts. **Sewage and rubbish** was left in the backyard, piled up in the street or thrown into open drains which ran down the roads. Even where there were drains and sewage pipes, they normally ran into the local rivers, – where people collected their water. In London, the Battersea sewer emptied into the Thames just above Chelsea's water intake.

A

Year	Population
1801	53,000
1811	62,000
1821	83,000
1831	123,000
1841	152,000
1851	171,000

SOURCE

The population of Leeds, taken from official census figures.

A view of Leeds produced in 1715.

B

SOURCE

SOURCE

Only 2,200 houses, inhabited by 12,000 persons receive water from water works. This is one in ten people. Sixty thousand of the population have no water except from wells and rainwater.

From the Commercial Directory of Leeds, 1834. A Commercial Directory contains a list of businesses and general information about a town.

D

SOURCE

By far the most unhealthy localities of Leeds are 'yards'. Some of these are airless from the enclosed structure and unprovided with any form of underdrainage. Ashes, garbage and filth of all kinds are thrown from the doors and windows of the houses upon the surface of the streets. The privies are few, open to view on both sides and in a filthy condition and often remain without the removal of any filth for six months.

Report by James Smith, a government commissioner, who investigated the condition of towns in 1845.

Edwin Chadwick

Edwin Chadwick (1800–90) was a civil servant. His job meant he had to investigate the causes of poverty in the towns. He wrote the report, *The Sanitary Conditions of the Labouring Classes* in 1842. This report revealed the true horror of living conditions of the poor.

A view of Leeds produced in 1846.

E

SOURCE

Diseases

Disease thrived in these conditions. The water carried germs; the rubbish and sewage attracted flies; the crowded rooms spread lice. The most common diseases were smallpox, scarlet fever, typhus, typhoid and tuberculosis. In 1831, a new one was added; **cholera** arrived from the continent. Further outbreaks started in 1848, 1854 and 1866. Cholera was very frightening. It could kill a person very quickly. The disease began with heavy vomiting and breathlessness. The skin turned blue, purple and then black; there was no cure. The cholera germ was carried in infected water – but this was not known at the time.

These were not only diseases of the urban poor. Wealthier people often had running water in their houses. But it came from the same rivers. Prince Albert, Queen Victoria's husband, died of typhoid in 1861.

H **SOURCE**

Class	Leeds (an urban area)	Wiltshire (a rural area)
Professional people	44	50
Tradesmen	27	48
Labourers	19	33

From 'A Report on the Sanitary Condition of the Labouring Classes', by Edwin Chadwick, 1842. It compares the average age of death in an urban and a rural area.

I **SOURCE**

Deaths from Cholera

Year	Deaths
1831	32,000
1848	62,000
1854	20,000
1866	14,000

Number of deaths caused by cholera epidemics in Britain.

F **SOURCE**

A cartoon from 1828 entitled 'Monster Soup'. It gives the artist's view of water from the River Thames, from which many Londoners took their water supply.

A Cholera Victim

The cholera starts with a fever. Vomiting or diarrhoea follows; the eyes sink; lips and face turn blue, purple then black. There are spasms. Then comes death.

G **SOURCE**

There is a dunghill which contains 100 cubic yards of filth. It belongs to a person who sells it by the cartload. The older the filth is, the higher its price. All food and drink must be covered: if left for a minute, the flies attack it and it is unfit for use from the strong taste of the dunghill.

A doctor describing Greenock in Scotland in 'A Report on the Sanitary Condition of the Labouring Classes', by Edwin Chadwick, 1842.

No.	When taken ill.	When died.	Where died.	Sex.	Age.	Occupation.	Circumstances.	Habits.	Any evidence of contagion or infection.	State of the Dwellings or Neighbourhood.
1	22nd August...	24th August ...	15, David square, Abercannaid	M.	36	Wife of Puddler (Welsh)	Very poor ..	Dirty	No possible contact ...	Damp, dirty, and unventilated.
2	22nd ,, ...	25th ,, ...	57, Quarry row, Tydfil's Well	F.	45	Wife of Fireman ... (Irish)	Poor	Dirty	ditto ...	Dirty, unventilated—yard at back most filthy.
3	23rd ,, ...	25th ,, ...	31, do do ...	M.	32	Fireman............... (Welsh)	Good	Clean and regular	ditto ...	A drain, which carries away house slops from houses above, runs under the house.
4	23rd ,, ...	26th ,, ...	13, Morris court, Merthyr	F.	75	Rag cleaner .... (Irish)	Poor	Clean	As a rag cleaner might have picked infected clothes	An untrapped gully at end of court, ash heaps of ashes steeped with excrement &c. House, no ventilation.
5	24th ,, ...	25th ,, ...	7, Cwm Canol street, Dowlais	M.	21	Hooker in Iron Mills (Irish)	Young Irish Labourer	Regular	No possible contact ...	Cesspool at back of house above level of lower floor—offensive.
6	24th ,, ...	25th ,, ...	1, Flag & Castle ct., Dowlais	M.	8	Son of Labourer (English)	Very poor ...	Dirty	ditto ...	Court unpaved, no convenience, earth sodden with house refuse.
7	24th ,, ..	1st September	16, Sunny Bank, Tydfil's Well	F.	53	Wife of Tailor ... (Welsh)	Very poor ...	Intemperate & Dirty	ditto ...	Cesspool in garden overflowing, floor of sleeping room thickly covered with dirt and filth.
8	25th ,, ...	27th August ...	1, Miles' court, Caedraw	F.	50	Wife of Hawker ... (Scotch)	Poor	Clean and regular	Her husband and herself travelled about the neighbouring towns—had been in Aberdare	Cesspool near house overflowing.
9	26th ,, ...	30th ,, ...	8, Coffin's ct., George Town	F.	80	Wife of Skinner ... (Welsh)	Poor	Very clean ...	Had attended her son, case No. 3	Unventilated—common cesspool in gardens full.
10	27th ,, ...	1st September	4, Lewis' square, Abercannaid	F.	32	Wife of Collier ... (Welsh)	Comfortable .	Clean and regular	Apparently spontaneous	Overcrowded with family and lodgers—9 out of the 12 attacked, 7 died. At back of bedroom heap of ashes foul with excrement.
11	28th ,, ...	1st ,, ...	9, Sunny Bank	F.	42	Wife of Labourer ... (Irish)	Comfortable .	Clean	May have visited case No. 7	
12	3rd September	5th ,, ,,	13, Mt. Pleasant, { Penydarren ...... {	F.	21	Wife and { of } Daughter { Collier } (Welsh)	Comfortable .	Clean	No known contact ... {	Unceiled cow shed under the house in a most filthy state.
13	6th ,, ...	8th ,, ,,		F.	8					

Official records of some people who died of cholera in Merthyr Tydfil in 1866. Did they all live in squalor? If not, does this mean cholera was not linked to bad living conditions?

Market Court in Kensington, London, in about 1865. This was typical of courts or yards at the back of crowded houses.

Working conditions

Working conditions in the towns also changed. Look at the number of **factories** in Source E. Factories meant many workers under one roof. For the workers, factories meant a loss of independence. Cottage workers had worked long hours, but they had decided when and how long to work. This gave them some control over their income. Factory owners demanded long and regular hours and set the levels of pay. Machinery was dangerous and injuries were common. Lungs became diseased from cotton particles or metal dust. Factory owners also employed women and children instead of men if possible. Women were paid half and children one third of a man's wage. **Women** and **children** had worked before, but in different circumstances. Shiftwork was new. Children had worked with their parents rather than supervisors who were strangers. There were, however, some good factory owners including Robert Owen, Richard Arkwright and Benjamin Gott.

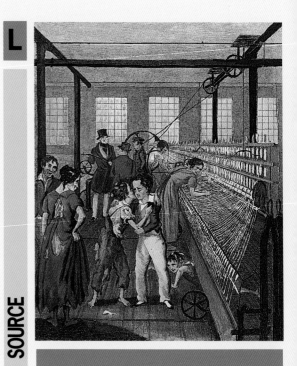

L
SOURCE

This picture appeared in a novel written by Frances Trollope in 1840. She was strongly against child labour.

M
SOURCE

When in the brisk time, did your girls go to the mill?
At 3 o'clock in the morning till 10 or half past at night.
What rest was allowed during these 19 hours of labour?
Breakfast a quarter of an hour, dinner half an hour, drinking a quarter of an hour.
Was any of that time used in cleaning the machinery?
They had to do what they call dry down; sometimes this took the whole of breakfast or drinking and they had to take food as they could; if not, it was brought home.
How long could they be in bed during those long hours?
It was nearly 11 o'clock before we could get them into bed.

What time did you get them up in the morning?
In general, my mistress got up at 2 o'clock to dress them.
So they had not above four hours' sleep?
No, they had not.
For how long together was brisk time?
About 6 weeks.
The common hours of labour were six in the morning till half past eight at night?
Yes
Were the children excessively fatigued by this labour?
Many times; we have cried often when they have fallen asleep with the victuals [food] in their mouths.

Had any of them any accident in consequence of this labour?
My eldest. The cog caught her finger and screwed it off below the knuckle.
Were her wages paid during that time?
As soon as the accident happened, the wages were totally stopped.
Have your children been strapped?
Yes every one.
What were the wages in the short hours?
Three shillings [15p] per week.
And in the very long hours?
An extra sevenpence-halfpenny [3p].

Samuel Coulson, father of two girls, giving evidence to the Committee on Factory Children's Labour, 1832.

SOURCE

One punishment is to cut off their hair close to the head, especially of those who seem most anxious to preserve it.

An anonymous pamphlet, 1837.

SOURCE

In Willenhall, the children are most cruelly beaten with a horsewhip, strap, stick, hammer, handle, file or whatever tool is nearest to hand, or are struck with the clenched fist or kicked.

Report of the Children's Employment Commission, 1843.

P

SOURCE

No man would like to work on a power loom. There is such a clattering it would make some men mad; he would be subject to a discipline that a hand-loom weaver can never admit to.

A worker giving evidence to a Parliamentary Select Committee, 1835.

R

SOURCE

The process of pointing pins on a grindstone can scarcely fail to affect the health of the operator; a portion of the brass dust will reach the mouths and lungs of the grinder; yet he takes no precautions.

A visitor to a Birmingham metal works in 1844.

Q

SOURCE

A chimney sweep and boy in the 1860s. Not all work in towns was done in factories. People worked in shops, markets and small workshops. But long hours and poor conditions were common. Sweeps sent young children up chimneys to brush out the soot. Sometimes they would get stuck or fall.

Mary Hootton

Mary Hootton was born in 1823. She went to work in a Wigan cotton mill from the age of eight. In 1833, she gave evidence to the commissioners investigating life in factories. She told them that Mr Swanton, the owner of her mill, punished her by tieing several heavy iron weights to her back whilst she worked.

The Poor Law

Most working people were poor by our standards. They had too little for a comfortable life. But lack of work or low wages made some people **destitute**: too poor to survive without help. These people were called **paupers**. Life was even more harsh for them. In 1834, the **Poor Law Amendment Act** was passed. It said that crippled or sick paupers should get **outdoor relief**, money or food in their own homes or special homes should be built to look after them. But **able bodied** paupers should be sent into **workhouses.** Workhouses were made harsher than the worst conditions outside. Families were separated. Work was monotonous; stone breaking and bone crushing were common. Uniforms had to be worn at all times, smoking and alcohol were forbidden and punishments for misbehaviour were harsh. The diet was enough to keep people alive but was mainly bread and cheese with occasional meat and vegetables. This **New Poor Law** was still in force in 1900.

Poor people shown waiting for help in the workhouse in a painting by Sir Luke Fildes, (1874).

T

SOURCE

Why were conditions so bad?

Why did living and working conditions like this come about? Were the landlords, employers and poor law guardians cruel? Why didn't the government step in to help?

One reason was **laissez-faire**, which was the idea that it was best if the government did not interfere in people's lives. This was a common view. People believed that the government should keep the country's finances healthy and control foreign policy. But it was not expected to look after individuals; they should do this for themselves. If government did interfere, they would make things worse. Local councils, therefore, did not have the power to control housing, water supplies and refuse disposal. Improvements would be expensive. Taxes would have to rise.

Another reason was **vested interest**. There were many people who profited from the growth of towns and factories. They included builders, landlords, water carriers, refuse companies and factory owners. They tended to argue against change to protect their rights. Even some workers argued against shorter hours and less child labour to protect their incomes.

What are the duties of the Government? To restrain crime; to protect person and property; to enact laws needed for order and justice; to sanction public works; to conduct relations with other countries. It is not the duty of Government to feed people, to clothe them, to build houses for them, to direct their commerce, to superintend their families, to supply them with physicians, schoolmasters. These are things people ought to do for themselves.

Edward Baines in a letter to Lord John Russell, the Prime Minister, in 1846.

We prefer to take our chance with the cholera than be bullied into health. There is nothing a man hates so much as being cleansed against his will.

'The Times', 1854, arguing against public health reform.

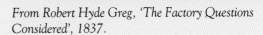

Our only advantages consist in cheap machinery and low rates of interest. By restricting mills, (with safety regulations, shorter hours for workers etc), we give up these advantages and hand them over to the enemy.

From Robert Hyde Greg, 'The Factory Questions Considered', 1837.

In a mill, the whole net profit is derived from the work produced in the last hour of the day. If the hours of work were reduced by one hour per day, the whole profit would be destroyed.

Nassau Senior, an economist, giving his opinion in 1837.

Extreme hardship would be inflicted upon tens of thousands of families in Lancashire and Yorkshire by a law fixing the hours at eight or even ten hours and absolutely forbidding the employment of a child for a minute longer.

From the 'Leeds Mercury', a newspaper, December 1831.

Factory Reform

During the 1820s some humanitarian factory owners such as **Robert Owen** and **John Fielden** alerted the government about working conditions. In 1830 **Richard Oastler** wrote a letter to the *Leeds Mercury* in which he claimed that factory workers were treated worse than slaves on sugar plantations. In 1831 a group of MPs formed the **Ten Hours Movement**. Their aim was to get the maximum working hours reduced to ten per day. **Anthony Ashley Cooper** (later **Earl of Shaftesbury**), an evangelical Christian, became the leader of the movement in 1832.

The government decided to set up a series of committees to investigate factory conditions. The official reports which followed revealed long hours, low wages and cruelty. In 1833 the first effective **Factory Act** was passed (see box). Four inspectors were appointed to check that the Act was being obeyed. This was an insufficient number, but at least it was a step in the right direction. The Act also showed that the belief in *laissez-faire* was beginning to weaken.

Under Lord Shaftesbury's influence, the government set up a Commission to look at the coal mines. The Commission's report shocked the country. Children as young as five were being employed for long hours underground. In 1842 the **Mines Act** was passed. The ten hour day in textile factories was achieved finally in 1847 (see box).

Public Health Reform

From about 1830, a series of campaigners and government reports publicized the filthy living conditions in the towns. In 1842 **Edwin Chadwick** published *A Report on the Sanitary Condition of the Labouring Classes*. This was packed full of information which showed just how unhealthy the towns were (see Sources G and H on page 42). When cholera returned in 1848, the government was stirred into action and passed the **First Public Health Act**. This was not very effective. When cholera went away, in 1849, there was less interest in cleaning up the towns. The Central Board of Health was abolished in 1854.

In 1867 working-class males in the towns were given the vote. It was clear they would vote for any MPs who were interested in improving living conditions. In 1875 the **Second Public Health Act** was passed. This made local councils responsible for public health. They now **had** to keep pavements lit, paved

---

Laws passed by Parliament

1833 Factory Act

- children under 9 not allowed to work in textile factories
- children aged 9–13 not to work more than 48 hours per week
- young persons aged 14–18 not to work more than 69 hours a week.

1842 Mines Act

- children under 10 and women not allowed to work underground
- fifteen inspectors were to enforce the law

1844 Factory Act

- all machinery to be fenced in

1847 Ten Hours Act

- maximum working day for young people under 18 and women to be 10 hours. [nothing was said about men]

1848 Public Health Act

- A Central Board of Health, based in London, was set up for a period of five years. It provided advice to Local Boards of Health.
- Local Boards of Health to be set up in towns with a high death rate or where 10% of the ratepayers demanded it. [Many towns did not bother to set up a Board of Health.]
- Local Boards could clean streets, provide water and sewerage - but this was **not** compulsory.

'Liverpool Quay by Moonlight', painted by John Atkinson Grimshaw in 1887. This busy street in the docks area of a large town is paved, clean, drained and well lit.

and cleaned, sewers clean and rubbish clear from the streets. They raised the money from ratepayers. Another reform in 1875 was the **Artisans' Dwellings Act**. This gave councils power to clear slums and build better housing.

Conclusion

There were also other improvements for working people. The period from 1840 to 1870 was a successful one for British industry. Many people's wages began to rise faster than prices and there was less unemployment. More hospitals were built and doctors learned how to prevent infectious diseases. The death rate began to fall.

Despite this, there were still many jobs with long hours and low wages. There were no old age pensions. Old people who could not support themselves had to go into the workhouse. There were still many slums. Further improvements in living and working conditions were to follow after 1900.

Shaftesbury

Anthony Ashley Cooper (1801–85), Lord Ashley, later became Lord Shaftesbury. He was an Evangelical Christian. He led the Ten Hours Movement to limit the working day and helped apprentices, mine workers and 'climbing boys' who were sent up chimneys to clean them. He was on the Board of Health set up in 1848 to improve living conditions and was President of the Ragged Schools Union for poor children.

3.1 Trade

In 1750 Britain was a leading trading nation . The main ports included London, Liverpool, Bristol, Glasgow and Hull. The whole nation benefited from trade. It brought wealth to Britain's 6,000 traders; it employed about 100,000 seamen. Traders helped to finance road, canal and railway building. The government also benefited; it taxed imports and exports and spent the income to strengthen the army and navy.

Trade was so important that the government used taxes to control it. The idea was to make sure that Britain benefited as much as possible and to obstruct trading rivals such as France and Spain. High taxes on some imports protected British manufacturers from foreign competition. This is called a **protectionist** policy.

British trading companies set up bases in many parts of the world. Sometimes, for example, in India, they used armies to force foreign rulers to trade with Britain. Sometimes these places were forced to become British colonies.

The dockside in the port of Bristol in 1720. The wealthy traders in the foreground were useful as investors. One Gateshead merchant traded in sugar, chocolate, tea and tobacco. He was also the biggest producer of salt in the country and owned coalmines.

Trade with the colonies was protected to benefit Britain. **Navigation Laws** forced British colonies to buy manufactured goods only through Britain and send their products, such as sugar, cotton, clay and tobacco to Britain only in British or colonial ships.

But not everyone agreed with protectionism. In 1776, Adam Smith, a Scottish economist, wrote a book called the *Wealth of Nations*. He argued that trade laws and trade taxes only hindered trade. British manufacturers began to agree with him. By 1840, Britain was the world's leading manufacturer; its industries no longer needed protection. The government adopted **Free Trade** policies, which reduced or abolished taxes on trade. This meant that foreign goods like tea, coffee, sugar and, later, frozen meat became cheaper in Britain. This was good for the British public. It also enabled manufacturers to buy cheaper raw materials and it encouraged countries who sold Britain raw materials to buy British manufactured products in return. This boosted trade.

By 1870, Britain's exports were still bigger than than those of Germany, France and Italy put together and over three times as big as those of the United States. However, after 1870 there were signs of trouble. German and American exports were growing faster than Britain's. Britain's imports were greater than its exports. By 1900, there was a growing demand for a return to protection to reduce imports.

From an article, entitled 'Made in Germany', written in 1896 by E. E. Williams.

Adam Smith

Adam Smith (1725–90) was a Glasgow University professor. In 1776, he wrote a book called *The Wealth of Nations*. He wrote that all nations would be more wealthy if each nation exported the goods it made most cheaply and imported goods which others made more cheaply. He said that taxes on trade got in the way of this free exchange of goods. The Younger Pitt, Sir Robert Peel and William Gladstone were Prime Ministers who followed Smith's idea of *free trade*. By 1860, Britain's trading policy was based firmly on free trade.

C

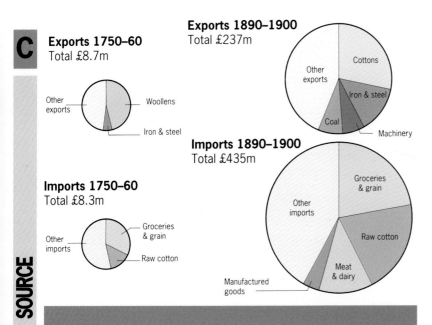

Exports 1750–60
Total £8.7m

Exports 1890–1900
Total £237m

Imports 1750–60
Total £8.3m

Imports 1890–1900
Total £435m

SOURCE

British imports and exports, 1750s and 1890s (average annual figures for each decade).

3.2 Empire

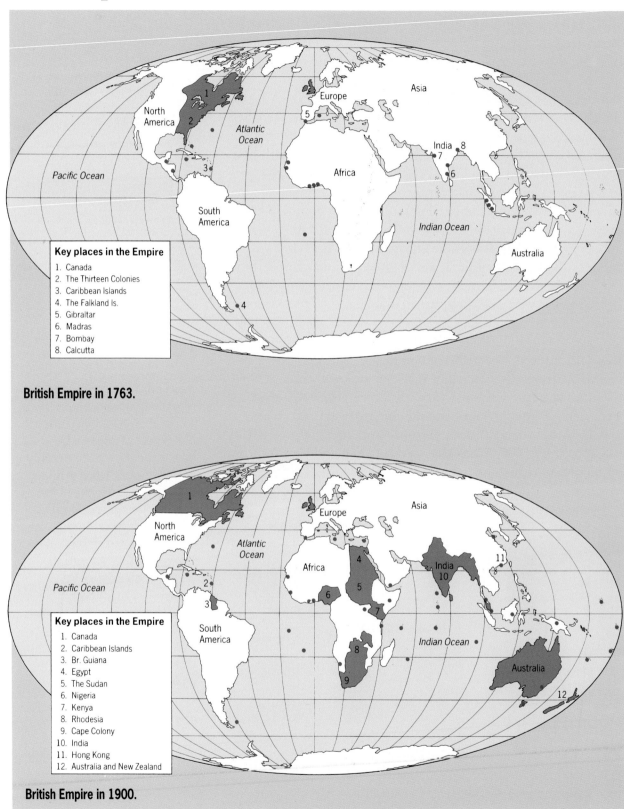

Key places in the Empire

1. Canada
2. The Thirteen Colonies
3. Caribbean Islands
4. The Falkland Is.
5. Gibraltar
6. Madras
7. Bombay
8. Calcutta

British Empire in 1763.

Key places in the Empire

1. Canada
2. Caribbean Islands
3. Br. Guiana
4. Egypt
5. The Sudan
6. Nigeria
7. Kenya
8. Rhodesia
9. Cape Colony
10. India
11. Hong Kong
12. Australia and New Zealand

British Empire in 1900.

By 1763, Britain was a leading colonial power. Some colonies were the **spoils of war**. In 1713 and 1763, Britain took land in Canada and the West Indies from France. Other colonies were set up by British **settlers**. Britons had been settling in North America, for example, since about 1600. Other British possessions were **trading stations**. The East India Company and the Royal African Company had set up trading posts on the coasts of India, China and Africa.

Over the next century the British Empire grew even bigger. Sometimes, to keep out foreign traders, the trading companies used their private armies to expand inland from their trading posts. This is what happened in India. Later, the **British government** used the army and navy to take over land to prevent countries like France and Germany getting it first. This happened in Africa and New Zealand. Some places, like Gibraltar, were taken as naval bases.

The colonies on the east coast of **America** and the **West Indies** sent sugar, tobacco, cotton and timber to Britain. But in the 1760s arguments broke out with the thirteen colonies in America. The colonists were fed up with interference from a parliament in London which they had no part in electing. They declared their independence in 1776. In the war that followed, the colonists were helped by France and other European countries. The War of American Independence lasted until 1783. The British army was unable to put down the rebellion. The colonies were granted their freedom in 1783 and the United States of America was born.

Britain fared better in **Canada**. In 1759, the British general, James Wolfe, captured the French fortress of Quebec. Cattle and wheat production made this a very prosperous area and many Britons emigrated to Canada. Its population grew to 3 million by 1865 and 6 million by 1900. In 1867 the Dominion of Canada was created, giving Canada more freedom to run its own affairs.

From 'Modern Britain, 1783–1964' by Richards and Hunt.

The British General, John Burgoyne, surrendering to American troops at Saratoga on 17 October 1777. British troops suffered further setbacks, notably at Yorktown in 1781, and eventually conceded defeat in 1783.

B

SOURCE

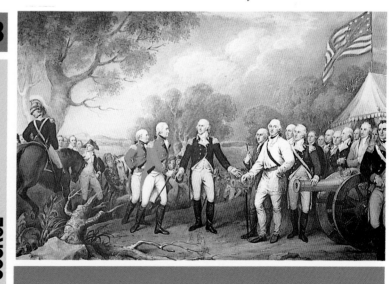

Britain gradually took control of **India**. In 1757, for example, Robert Clive gained Bengal from the French with a private army of the East India Company. Many of the employees of this company lived in luxury and took fortunes in salaries and bribes. Gradually, the British Government took over the powers of the company. The conquest of India continued. In 1857, Indians challenged British control in the Indian Mutiny. This was a rebellion which started amongst the Indians in the British Army. But the revolt was put down and in 1900 India remained firmly under British control. There was no increased freedom for India. Ninety-five percent of the senior jobs in the civil service remained in British hands.

SOURCE

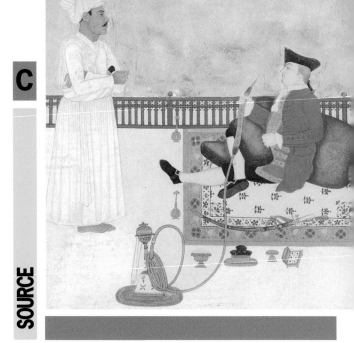

C

A British official of the East India Company, attended by his servant, takes a smoke, Indian style (1780). Some British travellers adopted the cultural habits of the countries they visited.

Captain James Cook claimed **Australia** for the British in 1770. They used it as a convict colony from 1788 until 1852. Convicts outnumbered free settlers until 1830. But farming prospered and in 1851 gold was discovered. Emigration from Britain increased; by 1914 Australia had a population of 5 million people and 100 million sheep. **New Zealand** became a British colony in 1840. Farming prospered there too, especially after the development of refrigeration enabled frozen products to be exported to Europe. Australia became a self-governing dominion in 1900 and New Zealand in 1907.

In 1850, Britain's main interests in **Africa** were two strategic areas, Cape Colony in the south and cotton-rich Egypt near the Suez Canal. Between 1880 and 1900 80% of Africa was divided up amongst the European powers. Britain took over control of sixteen colonies including Egypt, the Sudan, Nigeria and Rhodesia. This expansion was sometimes fiercely resisted by local people or settlers. British forces defeated the native Zulus and the Boers (former Dutch settlers) to achieve control of South Africa by 1902.

D

SOURCE

A 19th century Australian painting. Settlers in Australia took land from, and even hunted, the Aborigines, who lived there.

The British Empire brought **benefits to Britain**. The industrial benefits are discussed in unit 3.5. But British culture was also affected. Eating and drinking habits changed; tea, coffee and chocolate became common. Cheap wheat and meat were imported and the cost of living fell. Smoking became more widespread. Architecture also changed (see Source E). The wealthy wore silk and precious stones from the colonies. The British became proud of the Empire. From songs like 'Rule Britannia' and 'Land of Hope and Glory', we can get an idea of the patriotism inspired by 'The Empire upon which the sun never set'.

The **colonies** benefited from British influences in some ways. The British authorities built roads, canals, railways, schools, and hospitals. Some colonies became centres of Christianity. They inherited British laws, language and customs. But the colonies suffered too. British customs were sometimes forced on them and local customs, culture and religions were ignored. This was a factor in causing the Indian Mutiny. Local labour was often exploited; native lands were seized. If there was resistance, the British army usually suppressed it. Some local populations suffered badly. In New Zealand wars and disease reduced the Maori population from about 100,000 in 1815 to 35,000 by 1900.

Cook

Captain James Cook, (1728–79) was a navigator and explorer. He joined the Royal Navy in 1755 and served in the Seven Years War from 1756–63, during which he surveyed the St Lawrence waterway in North America. From 1768–71, and 1772–5, he explored the southern Pacific.

Cook enforced a diet which included fresh fruit and vegetables on his ships. This prevented scurvy.

In 1779, he was attacked and killed by natives in Hawaii.

The Royal Pavilion at Brighton, built around 1820, shows the influence of the East on British architects.

E

SOURCE

3.3 Emigration

In 1750, the number of people emigrating was small and roughly balanced by the number of immigrants. This remained true until about 1815. Between 1815 and 1900, 13 million people emigrated from Britain.

There were 'push' and 'pull' causes for emigration. Hardships at home sometimes **pushed** people abroad. Sometimes it was high unemployment, at other times high food prices. Overcrowded living conditions in the towns also persuaded some people to leave. There were two periods of very rapid emigration. One was during the Irish famine which began in 1846; hunger drove 1 million Irish to emigrate by 1850. The other was during the Great Depression in the 1880s when 200,000 people per year were emigrating.

But not all were forced abroad. Sometimes ambition **pulled** people abroad. The discovery of gold in California in 1849, Australia 1851, in the Transvaal in the 1880s and in the Klondike (Alaska) in the 1890s promised huge fortunes to a few dreamers. More realistically, the fertile and cheap land attracted many aspiring farmers to Australia New Zealand and Canada and the booming industries of the East coast of the USA promised rich prospects for the hard working.

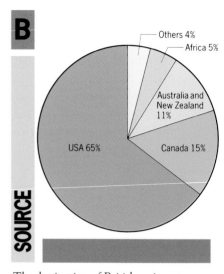

B SOURCE

The destination of British emigrants 1820–1900. Towards the end of the century, Australia and New Zealand were growing in popularity.

C SOURCE

FREE EMIGRATION TO SOUTH AUSTRALIA, via Southampton. Free passage to this healthy and prosperous colony to farm workers, shepherds, miners, mechanics and others of good character. The need for labour is urgent and will ensure the comfort of every man and his family.

An advertisement in the 'Northampton Herald', 1846.

D SOURCE

It cannot be doubted that the removal to Canada and other dominions of boys and girls from our workhouses might do much to relieve the labour market in this country.

From 'The Illustrated London News', 1866.

A SOURCE

An 1884 painting of immigrants just arrived in New York. Some made a fortune there, like J. J. Astor, who arrived penniless and died with $25 million.

There was no shortage of encouragement for emigrants. Poor Law guardians and the Salvation Army helped paupers to emigrate; trade unions had emigration funds for their members. The authorities in Australia and New Zealand were desperate for people. Railways and improvements in steam shipping also encouraged emigration by making long distance travel quicker, safer and cheaper than ever before.

A cartoon commenting on the government's policy of encouraging emigration in the 1820s.

We left Plymouth in February and arrived in Melbourne in June. We had six or seven deaths. Two dear women died in their confinement, one with an inflammation, the rest were children. We had plenty of food, but the little girls' teeth were not strong enough to eat the biscuits. The water got very bad. We found it very hot when crossing the line. We had one gale. Then we got into a cold climate. I was taken ill and was scarcely able to walk when I came on shore.

An emigrant writing home from Australia in 1849.

Decade	England and Wales	Scotland	Ireland	TOTAL
1830s	100,000	20,000	300,000	420,000
1840s	220,000	60,000	1,110,000	1,390,000
1850s	640,000	183,000	1,231,000	2,054,000
1860s	650,000	158,000	867,000	1,675,000
1870s	1,000,000	200,000	500,000	1,700,000
1880s	1,800,000	300,000	800,000	2,900,000
1890s	1,300,000	200,000	500,000	2,000,000

Emigration from Britain.

Astor

John Jacob Astor (1763–1848) was born in Germany. In 1779 he left his poor family farm and travelled to London. Five years later, he emigrated to America. He had almost no money, but started a fur business in New York which became immensely successful. He left a fortune of almost $25,000,000 and a legacy of $350,000 for a new public library in New York. He even had a town, Astoria, named after him.

3.4 Ireland

While the Empire was growing and Britons were emigrating all over the world, Britain was expanding in a different way. In 1801, Ireland was united to the rest of Great Britain. Thus, the **United Kingdom** was formed. Links with Ireland had never been happy and this new arrangement was no happier.

In 1750 Ireland was not part of Great Britain. It was a separate country, with its own parliament, but it was ruled from London by the British government. This had been the situation for almost 600 years. But Ireland was not ruled fairly. One reason was religious. Three quarters of the Irish were **Catholic**. Some of Britain's rivals, such as France and Spain, were Catholic. The government didn't trust the loyalty of Catholics, so it repressed them. It made the **Anglican** Church, not the Catholic, the official Irish Church. Catholics were banned from holding high office in government or the armed forces. Catholics were denied land. In 1800, Catholics owned only 15% of the land in Ireland. They had to rent from Protestant, often English, landowners.

In the 1790s, while Britain was at war with France, an Irish rebellion broke out, led by **Wolfe Tone**. The revolt failed, but it convinced the Younger Pitt, the prime minister, that the only way to keep Ireland loyal was to make it part of Great Britain. In 1801 Parliament passed the **Act of Union** which joined Britain and Ireland into the United Kingdom. The Irish got 100 MPs and 32 lords in the British Parliament. Their own parliament in Dublin was abolished.

Still Catholics were refused equality. It took the threat of a rebellion in the 1820s before the Duke of Wellington, the prime minister in 1829, passed the **Catholic Emancipation Act**, which gave equality to Catholics.

A SOURCE

Ireland 1844. There were almost no industries, there were very few towns, and not many farms were large enough to employ labour. It was a country of holdings so small as to be mere patches. The people lived in huts of mud mingled with a few stones, four or five feet high, built on the bare earth, roofed with boughs and turf sods, without chimneys or windows and empty of furniture, where animals and human beings slept together on the mud floor.

From 'The Reason Why', by C. Woodham Smith, 1971.

An engraving of a food riot in Ireland during the famine.

B SOURCE

In the 1840s, the union was put to the test when **potato blight** ruined the potato crops in Ireland from 1845 to 1849. Farming was undeveloped there; about two million people relied chiefly on potatoes for food. Although the British government tried to help, they did not do enough. Shortage of food turned to famine and disease. In the end, one million people died and 1.5 million emigrated. Irish opposition to the Act of Union increased still further.

In the 1870s, a terrorist group called the **Fenians** started a campaign of violence against the British. William Gladstone, the prime minister, tried to solve the Irish problems. In 1869, he took away the privileges of the Anglican Church in Ireland. He also passed two Land Acts in 1870 and 1881 to enable the Irish to buy the land they rented. But this was not enough. Inspired by **Charles Parnell**, the Irish demanded independence, or, failing that, Home Rule (a parliament of their own in Dublin to control domestic affairs). Gladstone tried to pass Home Rule; the Parliament in London overwhelmingly refused.

In 1900 Ireland was still part of the United Kingdom and still troubled. Since then, the southern part of Ireland has become an independent country, called Eire. Northern Ireland is still part of the United Kingdom.

'The Irish Whiskey Still', a painting by Sir David Wilkie, dated 1840.

Parnell

Charles Stewart Parnell (1846–91) led the campaign for Irish Home Rule. He was imprisoned for stirring up Irish unrest in 1881; he encouraged Irish farmers to boycott unfair landlords. He also encouraged Irish MPs to disrupt the work of Parliament with long speeches.

But, in 1890, he had an affair with Mrs Katherine O'Shea. His Catholic support faded; he lost all influence. He died in 1891, five months after marrying her.

3.5 Connections – Industrialization, Trade and Empire

Part Two of this book describes changes in population, agriculture, industry and transport which we call the Industrial Revolution. Part Three describes the growth of trade, empire, and emigration. All of these changes were **connected**.

Population growth was so fast that towns grew very crowded and unpleasant. This encouraged people to emigrate. Quicker, safer steamships made it easier to emigrate. From 1873–96, Britain suffered a depression. Unemployment in agriculture and industry encouraged emigration. Source A explains how the growth of population and unemployment also encouraged the growth of the empire.

During most of the 19th century, British industry was booming. Factories needed imported raw materials. Traders who imported raw cotton and clay helped the textiles and pottery industries. Traders also exported industrial goods. Britain produced 60% of the world's coal and half of its cotton cloth – too much to sell at home. Source C suggests that the need for raw materials and markets was one reason for the growth of the empire. Steam powered transport made this trade quicker and cheaper (see Source B). Some imports from British colonies started new industries. Tea leaves and coffee and cocoa beans were imported and turned into foodstuffs by new companies like Lipton's, Cadbury's and Fry's.

Trade provided money to help industry. Abraham Darby borrowed money from traders in Bristol to finance his iron works at Coalbrookdale. Josiah Wedgwood raised money from merchants in Liverpool to fund the Grand Junction Canal.

A **SOURCE**

I was in the East End of London yesterday. I attended a meeting of the unemployed. I listened to the cry of 'Bread! Bread!'. I became more and more convinced of the importance of the Empire. To save the 40 million people of Britain, we must gain more lands to settle the surplus population and to provide new markets for the goods produced by factories and mines.

Cecil Rhodes, 1895. Rhodes was a businessman who helped the expansion of white rule in Africa. He was Prime Minister of Cape Colony and then created the British colony of Rhodesia (now called Zimbabwe).

B **SOURCE**

'Oh where are you going to, all you Big Steamers,
With England's own coal, up and down the salt seas?'
'We are going to fetch you your bread and your butter,
Your beef, port, and mutton, eggs, apples and cheese.'

'For the bread that you eat and the biscuits you nibble,
The sweets that you suck and the joints that you carve,
They are brought to you daily by all us Big Steamers,
And if anyone hinders our coming you'll starve!'

An extract from a poem by Rudyard Kipling, 1911.

C **SOURCE**

When [an Englishman] wants a market for goods from Manchester, he sends a missionary to teach the natives the Gospel. The natives kill the missionary. The Englishman then arms in defence of Christianity, conquers for it and takes the new market as if it were a reward from heaven.

George Bernard Shaw, 'The Man of Destiny', 1898.

D

SOURCE

An Indian prince presents Robert Clive with the 'Grant of the Diwani' in 1765. This gave the East India Company the freedom to trade and collect money in that part of India.

Rhodes

Cecil Rhodes was born in 1853. In 1870, he went to the south of Africa to work on his brother's cotton plantation. He opened a diamond mine on his brother's land in Kimberley. Soon he owned several diamond mines and became one of the world's richest men.

His wealth gave him political influence in Africa. He had a vision of British land stretching from north to south across the whole of Africa with a railway from the Cape to Cairo to carry British trade. He forced Africans to give up their land, creating the British colonies of Bechuanaland (now Botswana) and Rhodesia (now Zimbabwe). He died in 1902 and left most of his wealth to Oxford University.

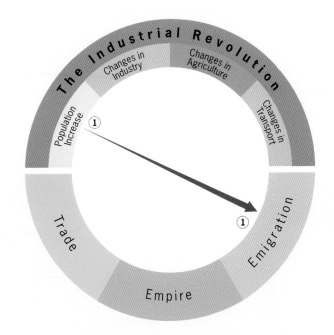

3.6 The Slave Trade: A Study in Depth

This study looks at how the Slave Trade started and how it was organized. It also covers how slaves were treated and the struggle to get slavery abolished.

Britain's most profitable trade route in 1750 was the '**Triangular Trade**'. Merchants bought manufactured goods such as cloth, pots and pans and guns in Britain. They loaded these into ships in Bristol or Liverpool and then sailed to the west coast of Africa. There, they traded with the chiefs of African tribes. The traders handed over their goods. In exchange they took African slaves. These slaves were crammed below decks for the six week voyage to the West Indies or America. This was called the 'Middle Passage'. The slaves were sold to plantation owners for large amounts of money, making the merchants a profit. The traders then bought tobacco, cotton or sugar from the plantation owners. These were shipped back to Britain and sold at a further profit. The ships then started the triangle again.

Equiano

1755 captured by slave traders
1766 bought his own freedom;
1797 died a free man.

The Triangular Trade.

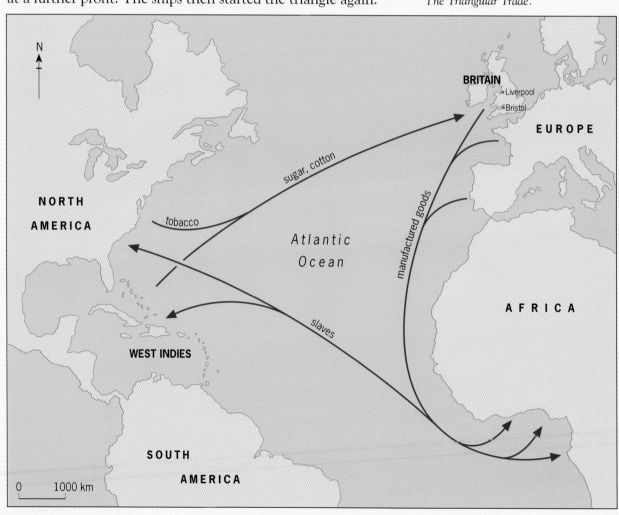

A romanticized French engraving showing European traders unloading goods on the African coast.

How did this trade in slaves begin?

European settlers set up colonies in America and the West Indies from about 1500. They grew sugar, cotton and tobacco on the fertile soils. But the plantations were huge and needed many labourers. At first, the only workers available were white settlers mainly from Britain, Spain and France. Few people made the dangerous trip across the Atlantic and many of these died of disease. In 1517, Spanish traders began to take African slaves and sell them to plantation owners.

British merchants saw the profits being made by foreign traders and wanted a share. John Hawkins was the first; he began to sell slaves to Spanish plantation owners in 1562. By 1673, there were 30,000 slaves in Barbados alone. The slave traders were making big profits. The profits were so large that governments helped their own traders. At the end of a war between Britain and Spain in 1713, the British government forced Spain to allow British traders to supply 4,800 slaves a year to the Spanish colonies in the Caribbean. This right was called the **Asiento**. As the number of British colonies in America and the West Indies grew, the number of British slave traders grew too.

From 1750, the slave trade was at its height. In 1764, there were 74 slave ships working from Liverpool and 32 from Bristol. British ships transported 50,000 slaves a year. At this time, Liverpool's ships alone carried 25% of the European slave trade. In all, the slave traders transported over ten million black slaves across the Atlantic. Over three million of these were taken in British ships.

Traders used the profits of slavery to help finance the Industrial Revolution. Liverpool merchants invested in great docks, canals, foundries, factories; in addition they underwrote Watt's steam engine, the construction of the Liverpool to London railway and the expansion of the Welsh slate industry. Slaving vessels also provided a steady source of trained seamen who could be conscripted by the Royal Navy.

From 'Black Ivory' by Charlotte and Denis Plimmer, 1971.

The Middle Passage

The slaves came from the west coast of Africa. Europeans didn't capture them. African tribal leaders imprisoned them. Some slaves had committed crimes; some were in debt. But most were captured in tribal wars. The African dealers held them in coastal prisons and sold them to visiting European traders.

The voyage across the Atlantic Ocean was terrible. The traders crammed as many slaves as they could onto their ships. Up to 700 slaves might be transported on one ship. Slaves were chained side by side onto shelves each with just 45cm of space. The hot conditions on board the ship were unbearable. Sailors had a saying that you could 'smell a slave ship five miles downwind'. Disease was rife. Captains threw infected slaves overboard rather than risk infecting their whole cargo. Even so, there was a high death rate.

The traders fattened the slaves like cattle in the final few days of the voyage. They also disguised sores with gunpowder and oiled their skins to make them look healthy.

C At first prisoners of war were sold into slavery. But later tribal leaders also began to sell law-breakers. One tribesman was sold for stealing a tobacco pipe. Another, who accidentally killed a man while shooting at a leopard, was not only sold himself, but so were his mother, three brothers and three sisters.

An extract from 'Black Ivory', by Charlotte and Denis Plimmer, 1971.

An early 19th century painting showing conditions below deck on a slave ship.

D

SOURCE

She had taken in 336 males and 226 females. The space between decks was so low that they sat between each others legs, so close that there was no possibility of their lying down or changing their positions day or night. This was when the thermometer was standing at 89 degrees [89F is 32C].

Captain Newton, describing conditions on his slave ship.

The slave deck was so covered with the blood and mucus which came from them in consequence of the flux [dysentery] that it resembled a slaughterhouse.

Alexander Falconbridge, surgeon of a slave ship.

Crews were often treated even worse than the Africans, for sailors were less valuable than slaves. If rations were short, the rule was slaves before sailors. In a single crossing aboard 'Alexander', all but three of the 50 crew were flogged, one man so often that he threw himself overboard.

From 'Black Ivory', by Charlotte and Denis Plimmer, 1971.

Hugh Crow

Captain Hugh Crow was a one-eyed Manxman who sailed slave ships to the Guinea coast for 18 years. He was a more kindly captain than most. He issued lime juice to crew and slaves to prevent scurvy. Scurvy was a terrible disease in which blood escaped from the veins causing ugly swellings all over the body and then death. On 27 July 1807, he was the master of *Kitt's Amelia*, the last slave ship to leave a British port.

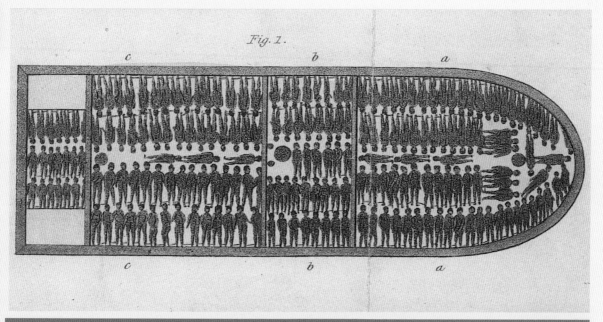

Fig. 1.

Plan of a slave ship, showing how slaves were crowded aboard. Some captains argued that more room saved lives; others said that the more you packed in to start with, the more you had left at the end.

How slaves were treated on plantations

Sometimes shiploads of slaves were sold in advance to one plantation. But normally the slaves were sold on the dockside to the highest bidder. In 1800 a strong male would fetch about £100; women and children were cheaper. James Madison, who later became president of the United States, calculated that a male slave cost him about $12 per year to keep and made him $257 profit with his work.

Most slave owners did not attempt to breed slaves. They regarded child rearing as a waste of time and money. So male slaves were normally kept separate from women; marriages were not encouraged. Many slave owners preferred to wear out their slaves with hard work and cruelty and see them die young. Buying new slaves was cheaper than supporting old weak ones. Slaves attempting to escape or start a slave uprising were normally punished by death. Runaway slaves in Jamaica, called **maroons**, set up villages in the hills. Some slaves were given their freedom; others committed suicide. All of this ensured that there was a constant demand for new slaves from the slave traders.

SOURCE I

Slaves hated the way they were treated. They sabotaged their owners by working slowly. They broke tools and let animals loose. Slaves pretended to be ill. Some slaves even burnt cane fields and owners' homes, or poisoned their owners. They were harshly punished for such behaviour. As well as whipping, slaves had their ears, noses and limbs cut off. Many slaves ran away.

Bob Rees and Marika Sherwood, 'Black Peoples of the Americas', 1992.

Slaves working on a sugar plantation in the West Indies in about 1823.

SOURCE J

Why did people support slavery?

In the 18th century, many educated people in Britain approved of slavery and the slave trade. They were almost completely ignorant about Africans. They rarely saw black people. Those portrayed in plays were clowns or villains. Traders exaggerated stories about African behaviour, with tales of polygamy and cannibalism. Since few people could understand African languages, misleading rumours spread. Many people believed that slave traders were helping the Africans by giving them the chance to become Christians and escape from their primitive life in Africa. Slave traders also argued that slavery was necessary to keep down the price of sugar and tobacco.

L SOURCE

God has approved of slavery and to abolish it would be robbery. Ending slavery would be extreme cruelty to the African savages, who are made much happier by it.

James Boswell, a Scottish writer and lawyer, about 1790.

K SOURCE

792   February 26, 1790.

RAN AWAY

FROM the subscriber, Two NEW NE-GROES, marked I in a diamond on the right shoulder; they are stout men, one a-bout 6 feet high, the other 5 feet 6 or 7 inches. Whoever delivers said negroes to THOMAS WATT, on *Lilliput-Hall Estate*, or W. & J. PATTINSON, *Montego-Bay*, or will lodge them in any Workhouse in this island, shall be handsomely rewarded.

JOSEPH JOBLING.

An advertisement in a Caribbean paper. Note that the slaves had been branded. This reflects the view that a slave was his owner's property, just like his cattle.

M SOURCE

The plantation owners do not want to be told that their Negroes are human creatures. If they believe them to be of human kind, they cannot think of them as dogs or horses.

Edward Long, 1774.

N SOURCE

It is impossible to allow that Negroes are men; because if we allow them to be men, it will begin to be believed that we ourselves are not Christians.

Montesquieu, the 18th century French philosopher and writer.

O SOURCE

The Negroe-Trade is a huge fund of wealth and power to Britain and is absolutely necessary for the maintainance of our Empire and other commerce in the Indies.

Malachy Postlethwayt, an English 18th century economist.

Thicknesse

Phillip Thicknesse, (1719–92) was a slave owner in Georgia and the West Indies. In 1778 he wrote, 'But surely they should be slaves, for do they not prefer a necklace of glass to one of solid gold and did they not fire on me with glass bottles from an ambush when I hunted them in the Blue Mountains with 50 or 60 soldiers?'

The abolition of the Slave Trade

The **Quakers** were the first to oppose slavery. They were members of the **Society of Friends**, a Christian group founded in the 1650s by George Fox. There were many Quakers among the settlers in America. Quakers treated everyone in the same way and believed that the holy spirit was in all humans, including slaves. They welcomed slaves to prayer meetings and asked owners to release slaves. However, progress was very slow.

Attitudes to slavery in Britain began to change after 1750. One group who opposed slavery were the **Evangelicals**. These were middle class Christians in the Church of England who wanted to see society organized by Christian beliefs. There were 20,000 black people in Britain in 1750. Many were slaves brought to England from the Caribbean. In 1772, **Granville Sharpe**, an Evangelical, raised this issue in court. The judge, Lord Mansfield, declared that no one could be kept as a slave in England. After this black people in Britain were free to follow their own way of life. This encouraged the campaigners. They decided that the best way to stop slavery in the colonies was to cut off the supply of slaves. In 1787, Quakers and Evangelicals combined to form the Committee for the Abolition of the Slave Trade.

The Committee wrote letters to newspapers, printed pamphlets and sent speakers to large rallies. They sought the support of politicians, cartoonists, poets and industrialists. They campaigned in the colonies as well as in Britain. William Wilberforce, an Evangelical MP, took the matter up in Parliament. But wealthy traders had a strong voice there. Twice proposals to abolish the slave trade were defeated. When war against France broke out in 1793, the prime minister, William Pitt, insisted that the issue be shelved. But circumstances changed. Pitt died in 1806. The British Empire was expanding fast. Traders now sent ships all over the world. The slave trade was less important than before. In 1807, Wilberforce demanded another vote. Parliament abolished the slave trade from May 1807.

Campaigners then turned to get slavery itself abolished. Slave owners complained that abolition would rob them of their property. The campaign made no progress. But, in 1830, a new government came to power which was in favour of reform. Slavery in the British Empire was banned in 1833. The slave owners were paid £20 million in compensation

P

SOURCE

A china medallion produced by Josiah Wedgwood in about 1790. Wedgwood supported the campaign against slavery. In a sense this was the first campaign button. It contains the words 'Am I not a man and a brother?'

Q

I had not seen among any people such instances of brutal cruelty. Might not an African ask you to learn from your God who says 'Do unto all men as you would men should do unto you'?

SOURCE

An extract from the life story of Olaudah Equiano, published by the anti-slavery movement in 1789. Equiano was an ex-slave. His book persuaded many people to oppose the Slave Trade. He travelled around England making anti-slavery speeches.

SOURCE

Mistreatment of slaves on the 'Middle Passage' was common. This cartoon was drawn by a supporter of the campaign against the slave trade.

William Wilberforce

William Wilberforce was born in 1759 into a family linked to Charles James Fox, a leading politician, and the Younger Pitt, prime minister after 1783. He was an Evangelical Christian.

Wilberforce was only 21 when he became the MP for Hull. His religious beliefs were the basis of his poitical life. He said slavery was 'a most detestable practice which shuts out light, truth, humanity and kindness'. He devoted his wealth and life to the abolition of slavery. He organized popular protests and used the support of famous names like Josiah Wedgwood. In 1807, parliament made it illegal for slaves to be carried on British ships.

The abolition of slavery in the British Empire passed its final vote in the House of Commons on 26 July 1833. By this time, Wilberforce was a sick man. Three days later, he died.

Politics in Britain and Abroad

In Britain in 1750, the **king** chose a **prime minister** to form a **government**. The government could only use policies the king agreed with, or he would replace them. The only limit on the king's power was **Parliament**. The House of Commons and the House of Lords had to vote on the king's policies before they became law. But Parliament rarely voted against the king. Parliament was dominated by landowners from the **upper classes**. The **middle classes** (business and professional people) and the **labouring classes** had very little say in politics. Most of them did not even have the vote. George III was king from 1760–1820. On the face of things, little changed. The king and the upper classes remained in control. But the political world around them was changing.

The American Revolution was the first sign. Colonists in the British Empire were not allowed to vote for MPs. But they had to obey the laws passed by Parliament. The colonists in North America thought this was unfair. In the 1760s, George III's ministers imposed new taxes on the American colonies. The colonists refused to pay. They said that they didn't elect Parliament, so they wouldn't pay Parliament's taxes. Their rallying cry was '**no taxation without representation**'. In 1775, these colonists declared war on Britain. The war did not go well for Britain. Eventually, Britain conceded defeat in 1783 and the colonists formed a new independent country, the United States of America. Their Declaration of Independence included the words '**every man is born equal**'. They believed that all the people should have a say in their government. If a ruler disagreed, the people could rebel and elect a new ruler. There was a message here for the people and the rulers of Europe.

The Political System in Britain in 1750.

A We hold these truths to be self-evident: that all men are created equal, that they are endowed by their Creator with certain inalienable rights, that among these are life, liberty and the pursuit of happiness. That to secure these rights, governments are instituted amongst men, deriving their just powers from the consent of the governed. That whenever any form of government becomes destructive of these ends it is the right of the people to alter or to abolish it and to institute new government.

SOURCE

Extracts from the American Declaration of Independence, 1776.

The French Revolution soon followed. In France, **King Louis XVI** chose the government. The States General, a parliament representing the people, rarely met. The government was very unpopular. On 14 July 1789, the Paris mob stormed **the Bastille** to release prisoners. Encouraged by their success, they swept on burning buildings and arresting ministers. The king and queen were captured and later beheaded. The people wanted a government which would give them '**liberty**, **equality** and **fraternity**'. Once again the people had taken control.

Some people in Britain wanted changes like those in America and France. **Corresponding Societies** exchanged ideas with the French revolutionaries. **Thomas Paine** wrote *The Rights of Man*, saying that the British government should be elected by all the people. This frightened the government. When Louis XVI was beheaded they were horrified. In 1793, Britain and other countries sent armies to France to restore the monarchy. The Revolutionary Wars dragged on through the 1790s. After **Napoleon Bonaparte** became the Emperor of France, they became known as the Napoleonic Wars. At last, in 1815, the Duke of Wellington defeated Napoleon at the **Battle of Waterloo**. A new king was crowned in France. Napoleon was defeated; but the revolutionary ideas were still alive.

B

Tom Paine tightening the corsets of Britannia. The cartoon was entitled 'Fashion before Ease'.

Wellington

Arthur Wellesley, was born in 1769. He joined the army in 1787. By purchasing promotions and with the help of family connections, he was a lieutenant colonel by 1793. After successful campaigns against the French in India and Portugal, he was made the first Duke of Wellington in 1814. He won his most famous victory when he defeated Napoleon at the Battle of Waterloo in 1815.

Wellington became a leading Tory politician and was prime minister from 1828–30. He died in 1852.

C

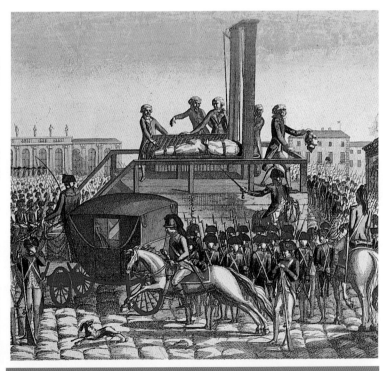

The execution of Louis XVI, 21 January 1793.

4.2 Power to the People (1)

In Britain in 1750, few working or middle-class people had the vote. If they wanted change they could not vote for new MPs. But there was plenty they wanted to change such as trade policies, working and living conditions, food prices and unemployment. They used a variety of methods to make their feelings known. Some were mild, like debating societies and demonstrations; others were violent, like machine-breaking and plots against the government. Before 1830 they were rarely successful. This was a period of popular protest and upper-class repression.

Some working people resented new machines which replaced skilled jobs, like hand-loom weaving. From 1811–12 there was a widespread outbreak of machine breaking by hundreds of workers known as the **Luddites**. An employer was killed at Huddersfield and a factory burned down in Wigan. In 1830, there were similar attacks on farm machinery all over southern England in the **Swing Riots**. The government used troops to put down machine breaking. In 1830, nine people were hanged and 457 transported.

Sometimes, middle and working-class people joined together in demonstrations. In 1819, a mass meeting was held in St Peter's Fields, Manchester. It was to be non-violent. Thousands of men women and children came with banners flying demanding 'Votes for All' and 'A Free Press'. Half way through, the magistrates decided that the meeting was illegal and sent in a troop of cavalry to arrest Henry 'Orator' Hunt, the main speaker. Angry protesters barred the way. Sabres were drawn and there was general panic. In ten minutes the field was

On 20 April a major fight took place at Middleton, where Daniel Burton's power-loom mill was attacked by several thousands. The mill was assailed by showers of stones and its defenders replied with musket-fire, killing three and wounding more. The army then met them and killed at least seven.

A newspaper report from 1812. The loom breaking was supposed to have been led by a man called Ned Ludd, but he probably no more existed than the so called Captain Swing who was supposed to have led the 1830 riots.

The House of Commons in about 1800. MPs were almost all wealthy members of the landed classes. They feared a revolution like the one in France in 1789.

C

A cartoon from 1819, showing the Peterloo Massacre.

Hunt

Henry 'Orator' Hunt (1773–1835) was a wealthy farmer with a wild background. He eloped with a friend's wife and was imprisoned for assault. He wanted the vote for all men and became a well known radical speaker. He was six foot tall and wore a white top hat. He had a bellowing voice. A contemporary said that when he was furious, his eyes were blood-streaked and stared from their sockets.

cleared, but 400 people, including 113 women, were wounded and 11 killed. People called it the Peterloo Massacre, a sarcastic reference to the Battle of Waterloo of 1815.

Working people started Britain's first trade unions at this time. The most famous was the **Grand National Consolidated Trades Union**. This was formed in 1834 by **Robert Owen**. He wanted the GNCTU 'in the first instance to increase wages and cut hours of labour'. But his long term aim was to 'create a new order of things and give the working classes more say'. This talk of power for working people frightened the government and employers. They opposed trade unions. Few lasted beyond 1835.

In 1820, there was a plot, called the Cato Street Conspiracy, to overthrow the government. This shows government officers bursting in on the plotters. The leaders were executed.

D

4.3 Power to the People (2)

The big question from 1830 to 1850 was who had **the vote**. In 1831 there were 16.4 million people in Britain; only 478,000 people, all men, could vote. They voted for 558 MPs of whom 400 were elected in the boroughs (towns). But these towns had been chosen in the Middle Ages and hardly changed since. By 1830, many were tiny; fifty boroughs had fewer than 40 voters. Appleby in Cumbria had just one voter. Some huge new towns, like Manchester, had no MPs of their own. This was so unfair that the smallest boroughs were called '**rotten boroughs**.'

There was no secret voting. People voted by a show of hands or writing their vote in a poll book. With so few voters, landlords could pay or threaten people to vote their way. The House of Commons was full of wealthy landowners. The working and middle classes had no MPs to speak for them.

By 1830, the demands for reform of Parliament had been building for 50 years. Meetings, demonstrations and riots seemed to be increasing. The government was frightended that there would be a revolution if there was no change. **Lord Grey**, the leader of the Whigs, the biggest group of MPs in Parliament, decided reform was necessary.

A **SOURCE**

The election for the borough of Finsbury took place on Islington Green. The clerk came forward and asked all those who were not allowed to vote to depart. Refusal to obey meant prison. But, as usual, no one paid any attention. The clerk then read out the name of a candidate and asked that candidate's supporters to raise their hands. He then read out the next name and so on. It is only fair to state that many boys and others who certainly could not be voters held up their hands. The Returning Officer then declared that Mr. Wakeley and Mr. Grant had been elected. Uproar followed. Three candidates, Mr. Spankie, Mr. Babbage and Mr. Temple, demanded a poll. [This was where each voter had to prove his right to vote and record his vote in a register]. The Returning Officer agreed to this. The result of the poll was declared five days later. [Mr. Grant and Mr. Spankie were elected.]

Extracts from 'The Observer', December 1832.

B **SOURCE**

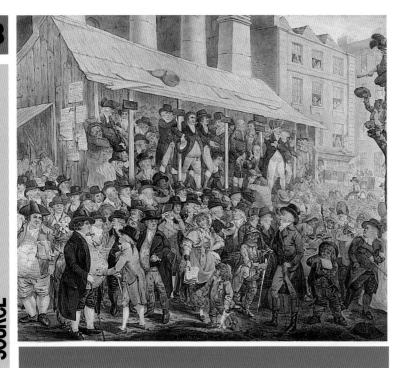

An election scene in London in 1796.

C SOURCE

A cartoon from 1832. The Reform Act took away MPs from 86 tiny boroughs and gave them to the big cities.

Grey suggested changes to Parliament in 1831. The House of Lords refused to agree. People were enraged. Riots broke out all over the country. In Bristol, rioters took control of the city for three days. King William IV was worried enough to threaten the House of Lords. He said that if they did not agree, he would create enough new lords to create a majority in favour. The threat was enough. The Lords agreed and, in 1832, the **Great Reform Act** was passed. It changed the rules about who could vote and moved MPs away from the smallest boroughs. The electorate, the people who could vote, almost doubled, to about 815,000. Most of the new voters were middle-class people. There was still no secret ballot.

After 1832, reform continued. Laws were passed to make electing local councils fairer, to improve schools and working conditions, to make poor relief cheaper and improve the banking system. Middle–class people liked the reforms. But working people were desperately disappointed. (see Unit 4.8). They did not think the new laws helped them. They still did not have the vote. Power stayed in the hands of the middle and upper classes for many more decades.

William IV

William was born in 1765, the third son of George III.

He trained as a sailor and served in the Royal Navy in the wars against the American colonies, 1776–83. In the navy, he became close friends with Viscount Nelson.

In 1830, his brother, George IV, died without children and William became king at the age of 64. He supported the Reform Bill because he believed that if the government refused a new voting system, a revolution could overthrow the government and the monarchy.

D SOURCE

It is safe to say that the Act did nothing for the working classes, in spite of their enthusiastic support for reform. It was the factory owners rather than the factory workers who benefited. Only about 400,000 new voters were added. In other words, the landed gentry had merely shared a little of its political power with the new industrial and commercial middle class.

From 'Britain Since 1700', by R.J. Cootes, 1968.

E SOURCE

1832 was a turning point in British history. It opened the way for social reforms over the next few years. It began a long period of middle class control of Parliament. It set the precedent for later Reform Acts which gave the vote to workers in 1867 and the whole adult population by 1828. Its greatest service to the British people was to prevent a revolution.

From 'A Survey of British History', by C.P. Hill, 1968.

4.4 Power to the People (3)

After 1850 the working class gained more political influence. Their first successes were with **New Model Trade Unions**. These were unions for skilled workers. They charged fairly high subscriptions which were used to provide benefits like sickness and unemployment payments to their members. They were very moderate. They didn't threaten to destroy industry, they negotiated with employers for improvements. There were very few strikes. By 1865 one such union, the Amalgamated Society of Engineers, had 30,000 members.

Union leaders began to meet politicians to argue that working men should have the vote. The new political leaders, like **William Gladstone**, a Liberal, and **Benjamin Disraeli**, a Conservative, could see that working people could be trusted with a share of power. They were impressed by their organization and moderation. In 1867, the Tory government passed the **Second Reform Act**.

This Act increased the electorate from about 1.5 million to about 2.5 million. The new voters were the better off workers in the towns. In 1872, the Ballot Act was passed by the Liberal Party. This made voting secret; it was now possible for people to vote without worrying about threats from their landlords or employers. In 1884 the Third Reform Act gave more working people the vote. The electorate rose to about 5 million out of a population of 30 million. Parliament now had to listen to the needs of the working class. New laws, such as the **Public Health Act** of 1875, improved their living conditions.

But there were still many working people without the vote. They needed another way to make their voices heard. This led to the **New Unions**. These were trade unions for unskilled labourers, like dockers and railway workers. They had low subscriptions, and they weren't interested in side benefits.

A **SOURCE**

Every man who is not incapacitated by some personal unfitness or political danger is morally entitled to come within the pale of the constitution.

Gladstone's attitude to the vote in 1864.

B **SOURCE**

His virtue, prudence, intelligence and frugality entitle him to enter the privileged pale of the constituent body of the country.

Disraeli describing the skilled working class in 1860.

C **SOURCE**

A New Model Union membership card. It tells us a lot about the image of the skilled working classes by 1870.

I do not believe in sick pay, out of work pay and other pays. The thing to do is firstly to organize, then reduce hours of labour and that will prevent illness and members out of work.

Will Thorne, leader of the Gas Workers' Union, 1889.

Besant

Anne Besant (1847–1933) was an early British socialist. In 1875, she was prosecuted for advocating birth control for women.

In 1888, Annie Besant organized a strike for more pay and better working conditions for women at the Bryant and May matchworks in London. These women earned just one penny a week making matches using phosphorous on the head. Phosphorous caused an illness called 'phossy jaw'. The strike was the first success for the New Unions.

'The British Beehive' an 1840 engraving re-issued in 1867 as part of the campaign for the 1867 Reform Act. It has a clear message about British society by the middle of the 19th century.

They set out to *force* employers to increase wages. The dockers' strike forced an increase in pay in 1889. By 1900 there were 2 million members of New Unions.

These unions began to work with the few working class MPs, like **Keir Hardie**. They wanted a stronger voice in Parliament for the working class. In 1900, they formed the **Labour Representation Committee** to help working-class candidates for Parliament. In 1906, 29 LRC candidates were elected. They decided to call themselves the **Labour Party**.

By 1900 the monarch had very little real power. The landowners still dominated the House of Lords and provided many government ministers, but they shared power in the Commons with the middle-classes. Many working men also had the vote as well as the support of unions and the Labour Party. Women still had no say in politics.

E

A PENNY POLITICAL PICTURE FOR THE PEOPLE,
WITH A FEW WORDS UPON PARLIAMENTARY REFORM.
BY THEIR OLD FRIEND, GEORGE CRUIKSHANK

4.5 Gladstone and Disraeli

William Ewart Gladstone was born in Liverpool in 1809. He was a Christian who nearly chose the Church as a career; he saw politics in moral terms, a matter of doing what was right. He was educated at Eton and Oxford University.

Gladstone became a Tory MP in 1832, Under Secretary for the Colonies in 1835 and then President of the Board of Trade in 1843. There was a split in the Tory Party in 1846 and Gladstone left, eventually joining the Liberals. He was Chancellor of the Exchequer 1852–55 and 1859–65 and Prime Minister four times, 1868–74, 1880–85, 1886 and 1892–94.

Gladstone increased the number of working men with the vote, modernized schools, the army and the civil service and passed social reforms to help the poor. He opposed expansion of the Empire and wanted to give Ireland more independence.

He was famous for his hard work and lengthy speeches. He had no patience with his opponents. He was never popular with Queen Victoria. The public were fond of 'The Grand Old Man's' social reforms, but not his foreign or Irish policies. He died in 1898.

Benjamin Disraeli was born in 1804. His father was a wealthy Jewish writer. Disraeli was notorious in his youth for his colourful clothes and gambling. He was a Christian, but he saw politics as a realist, a matter of doing what was best.

In the split of 1846, Disraeli stayed in the Tory Party. The Tories became the Conservative Party during this time. Disraeli was Chancellor of the Exchequer in 1852, 1858–9 and 1866–8 and Prime Minister twice, in 1868 and 1874–80.

Disraeli was the first to give working men the vote, in 1867. His Home Secretary, Richard Cross, passed many social reforms improving public health and working conditions. Disraeli was a strong supporter of the expansion of the British Empire. He made the Queen the Empress of India and his armies fought wars against the Zulus in southern Africa and tribesmen in Afghanistan to defend British colonies. Like most others at the time, he was strongly against Irish demands for independence.

'Dizzie' was a witty speaker who cut down his opponents with sarcasm. He flattered Queen Victoria and became her favourite minister. She made him Lord Beaconsfield in 1876. He died in 1881.

A

SOURCE

Caricatures of Gladstone (top) and Disraeli (bottom).

Typical of Gladstone was the **Alabama affair**. Britain was neutral in the American Civil War (1861–65). But one side bought a battleship, named the *Alabama*, from British shipbuilders. After the war, the Americans protested about the damage caused by the ship. Gladstone allowed an international meeting in Geneva to decide the dispute. Britain was asked to pay £3 million compensation. Gladstone agreed. This type of international co-operation became common in the 20th century but, at the time, the public were outraged that he should be so 'weak'.

Typical of Disraeli was the affair of the **Suez Canal shares**. The canal, opened in 1869, was the main sea route to the East. The ruler of Egypt owned most of the shares in the canal. In 1875, he went bankrupt. Without consulting Parliament, Disraeli borrowed £4 million from the Rothschild bank and Britain bought the shares. This bold act protected a vital trade route and was a typical example of Britain extending her control over less developed countries. The public were delighted.

The differences between Gladstone and Disraeli was shown by the **Eastern Question**. The Sultan of Turkey was a cruel and oppressive ruler who mistreated his subjects. But the Sultan ruled the Ottoman Empire, the only obstacle preventing Britain's enemy, Russia, from taking control of the Middle East. Disraeli, prime minister at the time, took the practical line and supported the Ottoman Empire. Gladstone, however, took the moral view. He campaigned for the breakup of the Ottoman Empire.

Gladstone

1843 – President of the Board of Trade
1852 – Chancellor of the Exchequer
1859 – Chancellor of the Exchequer
1868 – Prime Minister
1880 – Prime Minister
1886 – Prime Minister
1892 – Prime Minister.

Disraeli

1858 – Chancellor of the Exchequer
1866 – Chancellor of the Exchequer
1868 – Prime Minister
1874 – Prime Minister.

A cartoon from 'Punch', 1870, showing Disraeli (left) and Gladstone (right).

B

SOURCE

4.6 Education

In 1750, the wealthy sent their sons to **public schools**. There were nine of these; Eton and Harrow are the best known. There were no public schools for girls until after 1850. There were also about 100 fee paying **grammar schools**. Some boys went on to university. There were only two of these in England: Oxford and Cambridge; Scotland had four.

For poor children there were **dame schools**. These charged low fees, but they were often only somewhere for parents to leave children; they gave little education. There were also **charity schools**, like those run by the Society for the Propagation of Christian Knowledge. **Sunday schools** began after 1780 when Robert Raikes formed a Sunday school in Gloucester to give religious teaching to boys and girls.

The rise in the population after 1750, especially in the towns, made it obvious that there should be more schools. The government would not provide any, so the the Church of England founded the **National Society** in 1811 to provide schools for Anglican boys and girls. In 1814, the Nonconformist churches set up the **British and Foreign Schools Society**. These church societies used money raised by charity and charging small fees to build schools and employ teachers. **Ragged schools** – free schools, with very basic lessons, set up by individuals as acts of charity for the very poor – existed by 1844.

A **SOURCE**

I may truly say that I never learnt anything useful at Harrow, and had little chance of learning anything. Hours were wasted daily on useless Latin verses with sickening monotony. The bullying was terrible. Boys were sent out to bring back porter (beer), certain to be flogged by the headmaster if they were caught and by the sixth formers if they would not go.

Augustus Hare (1848), remembering his time at Harrow School.

Like the public schools, Oxford and Cambridge concentrated on Latin and Greek. No science departments were founded until about 1850. Many students, like these, wasted their time instead of studying.

B **SOURCE**

Present 170 boys; the room will hold 400. The only book in use for the upper classes was the Bible. There were no maps in the school. The children were taught nothing either of History or Geography. Indeed the master could not find time to give any direct instruction to the school, but was obliged to depend on his little monitors, not one of whom was 12 years old.

A government report on a church society school. The teacher was using the monitorial system, whereby he taught monitors and they taught the rest of the class.

C **SOURCE**

D

SOURCE

It would teach them to despise their lot in life instead of making them good servants. It would enable them to read seditious pamphlets, vicious books and publications against Christianity; it would render them insolent to their superiors.

Davies Giddy MP, in 1807, speaking in Parliament against education for the poor.

E

SOURCE

On the provision of education depend our industrial prosperity, the safe working of the constitution and our national power. If we are to hold our position among the nations of the world, we must make up for the smallness of our numbers by increasing the intellectual force of the individual.

E. W. Forster MP, in 1870.

G

SOURCE

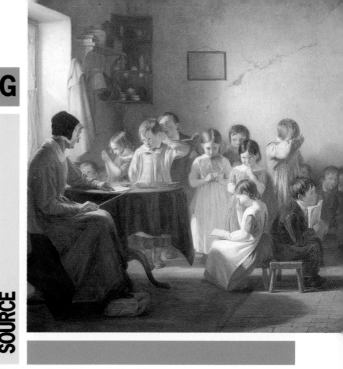

A dame school from a mid-19th century painting. Many women who ran dame schools had other jobs which they did as well.

Eventually, schools were helped by Government. In **1833**, the government agreed to give an **annual grant** of £20,000 to the two church societies. The grant increased until, by 1858, it had reached £600,000 per year. But there were still areas where there were too few schools. **Forster's Education Act** of 1870 gave ratepayers the chance to elect local school boards to provide extra schools. Elementary education became compulsory up to the age of ten in 1880 and free from 1891.

F

SOURCE

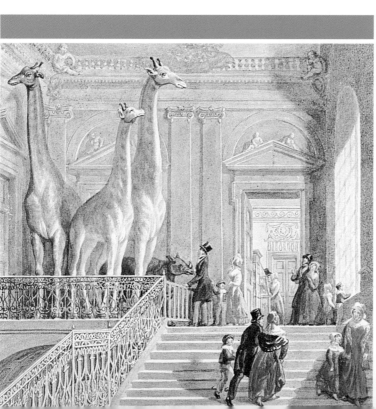

Lancaster

Joseph Lancaster (1778–1838) ran a school in Southwark. He created the **monitorial system**, in which a teacher instructed a small number of **monitors** who then taught the rest of the class. Under this system, £300 could finance a school for a thousand pupils. Andrew Bell created a similar system at the same time. Bell became the adviser of the National Society. Lancaster advised the British and Foreign Schools Society. Their methods influenced teaching throughout the century.

A London museum in 1845. Many people relied upon libraries, museums and evening classes to make up for the poor schooling they had received.

4.7 Connections – Politics and the Industrial Revolution

So far we have described changes in industry, population and transport and changes in politics in separate sections of this book. These changes were not separate; they were **connected**.

In 1750, most people worked in farming or skilled crafts. People were spread thinly across the countryside. They worked in small groups on farms or in cottages. They knew their bosses well. Most people felt that they belonged to their village, their farm or their craft. They may have felt a loyalty to their king and country. But people in one area of the country did not feel any bond with people in any other area. They would only know about their own district. Transport was slow and expensive. News travelled very slowly. As a result, there was very little interest in national politics. Sir Robert Walpole was prime minister for most of the 1720s and 1730s, but few people outside London would have recognized him.

During the Industrial Revolution, this changed. Industries grew rapidly around the coalfields, the iron deposits and the ports. Population there grew very fast. Big, crowded towns sprang up. People squeezed into houses packed around the factories. Hundreds of thousands of working people in the towns shared the same problems; poor housing and water supplies, disease, bad working conditions, low wages and unemployment. Bosses became distant, hated figures. Few workers could vote.

Cartoons and pamphlets were first to spread information about these problems. Famous political cartoonists of the time included Rowlandson and Cruikshank. The *Scotsman* was a newspaper founded in Edinburgh in 1817; the *Manchester Guardian*, (now the *Guardian*), was founded in 1821. By 1860, *The Times* was selling 70,000 copies per day. Railways took these papers around the country. People in different towns realized that they had the same problems. The working classes began to think of themselves as a group.

This working-class sense of identity had been made by the Industrial Revolution. It led to working-class movements like trade unions and Chartism. They realized that, if they worked together, they could force employers, and even Parliament, to listen to them. The working classes had entered politics.

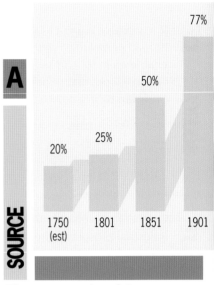

A **SOURCE**

77%

50%

25%

20%

1750 (est)   1801   1851   1901

The percentage of people living in towns.

B **SOURCE**

No other means are likely to be so effective as a combination of millions.

William Lovett, Chartist leader, 1840.

C **SOURCE**

Every industry was paralysed. The dock was crowded with vessels unable to unload or go elsewhere. The tremendous influence of the Union of Dockers will give the workers faith in themselves. Everything is possible in the future for the toiling millions of the mine and the factory.

'Reynolds News', 1 September 1889, describing the effects of the Dockers' Strike

D

SOURCE

A cartoon by Rowlandson, 1819, showing news sheets being sold in the streets.

E

SOURCE

This 1819 Cruikshank cartoon is a comment on the 'Six Acts', which banned large public meetings and controlled the radical press in an attempt to stifle any movement for reform.

F

SOURCE

Cruikshank

George Cruikshank was born in London in 1792. He was an illustrator and caricaturist.

He illustrated famous books of the 19th century, such as *German Popular Stories*, by the Brothers Grimm, and *Oliver Twist*, by Charles Dickens.

But he is best known for his political caricatures which both reflected and influenced political opinions of his day.

'Punch' cartoon, published in 1843. Called 'Capital and Labour' it shows the contrasts between rich and poor.

4.8 Chartism: A Study in Depth

The 1830s and 1840s were times of political upheaval throughout Europe. Governments who ignored the wishes of the people became more and more unpopular. Events came to a head in 1848. The French monarchy was overthrown and a republic with a president put in its place. This sparked violent unrest all across Europe forcing governments to make changes. Britain was the only exception. Here demands for political reform after 1832 came mainly from a mass movement of working people called Chartism. But the Chartists failed to change the government of Britain. This study looks at the causes of Chartism and the tactics used to try and get Parliament to accept the Charter. It also considers why, unlike pressure for political change in Europe, Chartism failed.

What caused Chartism?

The Industrial Revolution had brought sweeping changes to the lives of working people. Most working people lived in overcrowded houses with poor sewerage and contaminated water. Britain's first cholera epidemic broke out in 1831. Factory workers did not like the long hours, harsh discipline and monotony. Economic depression between 1830 and 1832 caused low wages. Many people could not find work at all. Unemployment was worst amongst skilled craftsmen like handloom weavers who could not compete with new machinery. The year 1830 also brought poor harvests and high food prices, causing starvation in the countryside.

Working people were not given the vote by the 1832 Reform Act. They were bitterly disappointed by this. The reformed Parliament did little to help the workers. In 1833, a **Factory Act** was passed to improve working conditions, but it was not very effective. In 1834, the **New Poor Law** was introduced but it was a cheap system, which put most paupers into harsh workhouses. This New Poor Law was hated, especially in the the north of England.

Working people were suffering and Parliament seemed only to make things worse. This is why Chartism started. It was a campaign to give working people their share of political power. But Chartists did not just want political power for the sake of equality. They wanted the power to elect a Parliament which would solve their problems and improve their lives.

A **SOURCE**

This question of universal suffrage, [one man, one vote], is a knife and fork question, a bread and meat question. By universal suffrage, I mean to say that every working man has a right to a good coat on his back, a good hat on his head, a good roof for the shelter of his household, a good dinner on his table, no more work than will keep him in health while at it, and as much wages as will keep him in the enjoyment of plenty.

Joseph Rayner Stephens, a Lancashire Chartist, saying how the vote would benefit workers.

B **SOURCE**

C **SOURCE**

Chartist leaders; Feargus O'Connor (top) and William Lovett (bottom).

The People's Charter, 1838

The Chartist movement was started in London by the **London Working Men's Association**. This was a group of skilled workers who met for discussions and political debate. The secretary of this group was **William Lovett**, a cabinet maker. In 1836 he met with **Francis Place**, a tailor sympathetic to working-class problems. They drew up a list of six changes which they thought would help working people. The demands were publicized amongst working people around the country, like the **Birmingham Politial Union** led by **Thomas Atwood**. These groups met at a mass rally in Birmingham in 1838 and other rallies were held in Liverpool, Leeds, Glasgow and South Wales. The demands were known as the **Six Points of the People's Charter**. Its supporters became known as **Chartists**.

D

SOURCE

Let us draw into one group the members of the working classes. Let us obtain a library of books which will inform us of our rights. Let us collect information regarding the wages, habits and conditions of the labourer. Let us publish our views so that we create a moral, thinking, energetic force in politics without violence or unrest.

A speech by William Lovett in 1836.

E

SOURCE

The Six Points
OF THE
PEOPLE'S
CHARTER.

1. A VOTE for every man twenty-one years of age, of sound mind, and not undergoing punishment for crime.

2. THE BALLOT.—To protect the elector in the exercise of his vote.

3. NO PROPERTY QUALIFICATION for Members of Parliament —thus enabling the constituencies to return the man of their choice, be he rich or poor.

4. PAYMENT OF MEMBERS, thus enabling an honest tradesman, working man, or other person, to serve a constituency, when taken from his business to attend to the interests of the country.

5. EQUAL CONSTITUENCIES, securing the same amount of representation for the same number of electors, instead of allowing small constituencies to swamp the votes of large ones.

6. ANNUAL PARLIAMENTS, thus presenting the most effectual check to bribery and intimidation, since though a constituency might be bought once in seven years (even with the ballot), no purse could buy a constituency (under a system of universal suffrage) in each ensuing twelvemonth; and since members, when elected for a year only, would not be able to defy and betray their constituents as now.

A summary of the People's Charter from a poster of the time. A seventh point, votes for women, was debated but rejected.

F

SOURCE

Many women were Chartist supporters. They formed their own Chartist groups, published pamphlets and marched in processions. Women were trusted members of the movement. Support for the idea of women's votes was widespread amongst male Chartists.

Dorothy Thompson, 'The Chartists', 1984.

The Charter

The Charter was born in 1836.

It went to Parliament three times, in 1839, 1842 and 1848. It was thrown out each time.

The Charter died in 1848. Of the six demands in the Charter, five have since become law.

Standing order of the House—
All members, not being able to stand or
sit, are ordered to lie under the table

A cartoon from the time by George Cruikshank called 'A Common's Scene'. This is what many people believed Parliament would look like if the Charter became law.

Chartist tactics

The problem now was how to get Parliament to agree to the Charter. In 1839, a **Chartist Convention** was held at Birmingham. Chartist delegates came from all over the country. They discussed how to tackle Parliament. Lovett and Attwood favoured **moral force**, that is persuading Parliament to adopt the Charter by peaceful means. But another group, led by **Feargus O'Connor**, an Irish journalist, favoured **physical force**, using threats, strikes, violence and even revolution. Other physical force Chartists included Bronterre O'Brien, Julian Harney and William Benbow.

The First Petition, 1839

Peaceful means were used first. In May 1839, a petition demanding the Charter, signed by 1,250,000 people, was presented to Parliament. It was rejected by 235 votes to 46. This caused a dilemma. What to do now? There was talk of calling a general strike in protest. But workers with jobs were not keen to risk them. The Convention could not agree on a strategy and it broke up having achieved nothing.

My desire is to use moral force as long as possible but I would have you remember that it is better to die free men than live as slaves. Physical force is treason only when it fails; it is glorious freedom when it succeeds.

Feargus O'Connor speaking in the early years of Chartism.

The Newport Rising, 1839

The Government took strong measures to discourage a possible uprising. In 1839 General Sir Charles Napier was sent to the North with 6,000 troops to guard against unrest. He paraded his men through the streets of large towns and invited Chartist leaders to displays of artillery fire to show the army's strength. In November 1839, a group of Chartists in Newport, South Wales, showed their frustration. They tried to take things into their own hands. They had been angered by the imprisonment of local Chartist leaders. Led by **John Frost**, they planned an attack on the town of Newport to release them. However, the authorities were ready. Magistrates had soldiers guarding their prisoners at the Westgate Hotel. Fierce storms reduced the number of protesters. When Frost and about 5,000 Chartists attacked the hotel on the night of 3–4 November, they were met with a volley of shots which left 20 men dead. One hundred arrests were made; Frost and eight others were transported to the penal colony of New South Wales in Australia. After this trade picked up and, as a result, Chartist activity declined.

I SOURCE

A cartoon showing a Chartist arming himself. He has a coal scuttle for a helmet and a dish for a breastplate. Did the cartoonist think that the Chartists were a match for the army?

J SOURCE

Welsh miners and ironworkers attack the Westgate Hotel in Newport. Despite their numbers, very few had guns; most were armed only with sticks. They were no match for the soldiers inside.

The Second Petition, 1842

In 1842, economic hardship revived demands for the Charter. The *Manchester Times* reported in July, 'Any man passing through the district will at once perceive the deep and ravaging distress that prevails, laying industry prostrate, desolating families and spreading abroad discontent and misery.'

By this time, O'Connor was the undisputed leader of the Chartists. In 1840, he had organized the **National Charter Association** which he hoped would unite all of the country's Chartist groups. By 1842, he claimed 40,000 members. With his fiery oratory and his Leeds based newspaper, the **Northern Star**, he had become the figurehead of the Chartist movement.

O'Connor organized a Second Petition. It had 3,317,000 signatures and was six miles long. It was presented to Parliament in May 1842. Fifty men carried the bundles of signatures at the head of a two mile procession of workers. But despite its mass support, few MPs supported the Charter. It was rejected by 287 votes to 49.

'Tour of Lancashire', 1842, by John Cook.

The Chartists take their 1842 petition to Parliament.

The 'plug plot'

Once again, rejection caused unrest. Lancashire cotton spinners were on strike for higher wages. Over 9,000 strikers gathered on Mottram Moor near Manchester. They demanded that the Charter should be adopted. Where other workers would not join them, strikers took the boiler plugs out of steam engines to disrupt their factories. This '**plug plot**' encouraged Chartist leaders to call for a **general strike**. They hoped that the economy would collapse and take the government with it. But few workers were interested. This was a key reason for the failure of Chartism. The authorities clamped down hard. About 1,500 men were arrested and 79 transported to Australia. By October the last strikers had been forced back to work. The depression lifted in 1843 and, as wages and employment rose, Chartism faded again. Moral force leaders criticized O'Connor's support for the strikers. Physical force Charists also criticized O'Connor. He was accused of threatening violence but being frightened to use it.

The National Land Company

O'Connor tried a new way of solving workers' problems. In 1845, he formed the **National Land Company**. It sold shares to workers in the towns and used the money to buy land. Shareholders then drew lots to see who would move to the countryside. In 1846 the first settlement began at **O'Connorville**, near Watford. By 1848 there were five others, including **Charterville** near Witney in Oxfordshire. But the plots were too small. The townsfolk made poor farmers. Funds ran dry and people drifted back to the towns. The scheme collapsed.

Thomas Cooper

Thomas Cooper was imprisoned for two years for supporting the plug plot. He supported Chartism from prison, writing verses to stir up support:

Slaves, toil no more.
Why delve and pine?
Slaves, toil no more.
Up, from the midnight mine.

An illustration from the 'Northern Star', 1846, showing O'Connorville. The 'Northern Star' was a mouthpiece for Chartist ideas. It had a circulation of 50,000 copies per week in the 1840s.

M

SOURCE

The Third Petition, 1848

In the winter of 1847–8, the economic depression returned. Unemployment rose. A **Third Petition** was organized. Chartists claimed 5,700,000 signatures. A huge rally was called for on 10 April 1848 at Kennington Common in London. O'Connor announced that 500,000 Chartists would march on Parliament with the petition. The government was alarmed and took strong measures. The Queen was moved to the safety of the Isle of Wight and the Duke of Wellington was given 100,000 soldiers to defend the capital. He also signed up 170,000 special constables. But heavy rain reduced the size of the rally to 20,000 people. Wellington refused to allow the march to Parliament. O'Connor backed down and told the crowd he would personally take the petition to parliament. The crowd dutifully dispersed. Upon inspection, the petition contained fewer than two million signatures, many of them false. MPs again rejected the petition, by 222 votes to 17. Chartist activity died away. It did not revive. Why was this?

The end of Chartism

Chartism grew out of hardship. But the depression of 1848 was an isolated one. After 1842 the standard of living of the working class improved. Railways boosted the economy; jobs and wages increased. Parliament passed a **Mines Act** in 1842 and a **Factory Act** in 1844 which improved working conditions. The **Repeal of the Corn Laws** in 1846 promised cheaper food. Working people also found other ways of making their opinions heard. Skilled workers set up the New Model trade unions to get better treatment at work. Co-operative societies started shops selling cheap food and clothes to workers. By 1850, there didn't seem the same need to change Parliament.

In some senses, Chartism was not a failure. All of the Six Points, except annual parliaments, eventually became law. The publicity which Chartism gave to the plight of working people helped other reforms, like factory reform. But most importantly, Chartism had given the workers a sense of class identity. It thus helped the growth of other working-class movements, such as the Labour Party and trades unions. Many Chartist leaders used their experience to help working people in local government or trade unions.

The honourable member for Nottingham, [Feargus O'Connor], stated that 5,706,000 names were attached to the petition. On the most careful examination this has been found to be 1,975,496. On many sheets the signatures are in one and the same handwriting. The committee also observed the names of famous people who can hardly be supposed to agree with the Charter's aims: among which occurs the name of Her Majesty as 'Victoria Rex', April First, Cheeks the Marine, Robert Peel and the Duke of Wellington [several times!]. The committee also noted a number of names which are clearly made up, such as 'No Cheese', 'Pug Nose', 'Flat Nose'.

SOURCE

From a Report of the House of Commons, 13 April 1848.

SOURCE

A 'Punch' cartoon commenting on the strange names on the petition. Notice that the Duke of Wellington appears several times just as his name did on the petition.

An engraving of the 1848 Kennington Common meeting.

Feargus O'Connor

Feargus O'Connor was born in Ireland in 1796. He was briefly MP for County Cork in 1832. He paid reporters three guineas to report his speeches. After he became a Chartist, he started his own newspaper, the *Northern Star*, which sold 50,000 copies per week from its base in Leeds by 1842. His oratory and his newspaper made O'Connor the most famous Chartist leader.

But O'Connor was a poor leader. One year, he made £13,000 profit from the paper; but he spent wildly and often could not pay the printers. His **Land Scheme** was badly organized. The subscribers paid £100,000; of this only £45,000 was spent on land and buildings; the rest was squandered.

O'Connor claimed to be a physical force Chartist. In 1839 he told one meeting, 'Physical force is only treason when it fails'. But he never really believed that Charists could win by force. He said they should, never be so foolish as to bare their naked bodies to disciplined soldiers. He was also more frail than his huge size suggested. By the 1848 rally, he was very ill. He had not slept for six nights and had a severe pain in his chest caused by nervousness. He blustered about force, but he never intended to use it.

O'Connor became even more ill after 1848. His wild red hair turned white; from 1852 he became insane. He died, penniless, in 1855. Over 30,000 people attended his funeral.

5.1 Britain in 1900 – so far from 1750

After 1750, Britain had the world's first industrial revolution. By 1900 it was still the most powerful industrial and trading nation, though others were catching up fast. Steam powered machinery had increased output and changed working conditions. Some old skilled crafts had disappeared. The population had grown from 7 to 37 million. The extra people provided the demand and the workers for industry and had created huge industrial cities like Manchester, Glasgow and Birmingham. They had thousands of factories and millions of crowded terraced houses. Gradually, they got water supplies, sewerage, schools and churches too. Farmers had found ways of producing enough food to feed the cities, using fewer workers. Horse power had been joined by steam power and petrol.

During this time, too, Britain tried to create a new relationship with Ireland; lost its American colonies; and gained the biggest empire in the world. Britain exported more than any other nation, including over 13 million Britons (the equivalent of 20% of the whole population of Britain today), who emigrated abroad. Imperial rivalry was causing friction between Britain, France and Germany.

'Work' an 1863 painting by Ford Madox Brown. The Victorians saw hard work as a virtue. This painting makes the point that the townspeople, the bookish gentlemen looking on, the children and even the poor street seller all depend on the work of the six heroic navvies at the centre of the painting.

SOURCE A

By 1900 many British people enjoyed travelling by railway to the seaside, with its jellied eels, bathing machines and Punch and Judy on the beach. They might visit a travelling circus or, in the evenings, one of the music halls that existed in all the major towns. Public houses flourished, horse racing, cricket and boxing were at least as popular as they had been a century before and had been joined by league soccer, the greatest of all mass sports. Cock-fighting and badger-baiting continued in the 1880s but the RSPCA was campaigning against them. Thomas Hardy, Emily Bronte and Charles Dickens were great Victorian authors; Bernard Shaw and Oscar Wilde playwrights; Constable and Turner artists.

By 1900 it was possible to send telegrams to America through a trans-Atlantic cable laid in 1865 and to speak on the telephone, invented in 1876. Gramophones first appeared in 1877, and radios in 1896. Dynamite and machine guns had been around since 1867, typewriters since 1874, and the first movies since 1895. Doctors used blood transfusions, anaesthetics, like chloroform, and antiseptics, like carbolic acid, though penicillin and the National Health Service were still almost 50 years away. People opened tins of Heinz food from America, or possibly asked their cooks, maids or butlers to.

By 1900 the first primitive electric vacuum cleaners, kettles, washing machines and dishwashers had arrived. Yet 20,000 homeless people lived in London's streets. Amelia Bloomer had designed the first trousers for women in 1862, but they still could not vote. Men were wearing top hats; but underclothes were still rare among the poor. Some streets were lit with gas or electric lights. Finally, as befits a year which sits astride the old Britain and the new, London in 1900 had thousands of new petrol driven motor buses but Londoners also used 116,000 horses which produced almost half a million tons of manure a year.

The first section of the London Underground opened as early as 1863. Locals called it 'The Sewer'. This poster is dated 1910; it shows us styles of dress in about 1900 as well as the interest in travel for leisure.

Queen Victoria

Queen Victoria (1819–1901) became Queen at the age of 18. The monarchy was not popular; she survived seven assassination attempts. In 1840, she married Albert of Saxe-Coburg; they had nine children. They became popular, living moral decent lives, unlike monarchs. Albert supported some social reforms and helped to plan the Great Exhibition of 1851.

When Albert died of typhoid fever in 1861, Queen Victoria avoided public life for a while. Disraeli encouraged her to be more active. When she died, she was revered by her people.

5.2 Britain in 1900 – So close to today

The Britain in which we live today is the product of the events you have studied in this book. Sometimes things from the past remain as relics, like factories preserved for the public to visit. Sometimes, despite their age, 19th century things remain in use, more or less as they were, like the Houses of Parliament. Sometimes things from the past have evolved into modern versions, like modern cars. Some things from the past have disappeared, like the slave trade in Britain. But even these leave traces, like the size of the Liverpool docks.

You can still see factories, the chimneys and the pit-heads which are the remains of the Industrial Revolution. Steam power has passed. But gas and electrical power still competes with nuclear power in industry. You can still see the canals, the railways and the docks built over a hundred years ago. If you look carefully, you can even see toll-houses from the turnpike trusts. More obvious signs of the transport revolution are the bicyles, cars, lorries and aeroplanes. All of these began life in the late 19th century.

Because of the agricultural revolution, very few of us grow our own food. The number of farmers continues to fall as farm machinery continues to increase and we import more and more of our food. Population growth has now slowed down; but the increases of the 19th century mean that most of us still live in crowded towns. Almost all of today's great cities grew up in the first half of the 19th century. Many of them still have great public buildings from their days of industrial prosperity.

The United Kingdom remains a union of England, Scotland, Wales and part of Ireland. As Britain's industrial strength has declined, so has its power in the world. The great British Empire is gone. But you can still see the effects of it. Britain still heads a family of nations called the Commonwealth, based on ex-colonies. Immigration from parts of the Empire has given modern Britain a multi-cultural population.

Finally, politics today still show the effects of the past. Britain is still a constitutional monarchy. The monarch still has a few carefully controlled political powers. Parliament still sits in the same buildings as in Queen Victoria's time. The prime minister, the cabinet and MPs, and large political parties still dominate Britain as they did a hundred years ago. Trade unions still represent workers. The main change is that women now have the vote.

2000 AD

By the year 2000, of all the things described in this book:
- some will have disappeared
  – like the Chartists
- some will remain as relics
  – like derelict factories
- some will remain intact
  – like the Houses of Parliament
- some will evolve into new forms
  – like modern cars.